Better Homes and Gardens.

# Cooking with Whole Grains

## BETTER HOMES AND GARDENS® BOOKS

Editor: Gerald M. Knox
Art Director: Ernest Shelton
Managing Editor: David A. Kirchner

Food and Nutrition Editor: Nancy Byal
Department Head, Cook Books: Sharyl Heiken
Associate Department Heads: Sandra Granseth,
    Rosemary C. Hutchinson, Elizabeth Woolever
Senior Food Editors: Julie Henderson, Julia Malloy,
    Marcia Stanley
Associate Food Editors: Jill Burmeister, Molly Culbertson,
    Linda Foley, Linda Henry, Joyce Trollope, Diane Yanney
Recipe Development Editor: Marion Viall
Test Kitchen Director: Sharon Stilwell
Test Kitchen Home Economists: Jean Brekke, Kay Cargill,
    Marilyn Cornelius, Maryellyn Krantz, Dianna Nolin,
    Marge Steenson

Associate Art Directors: Linda Ford Vermie, Neoma Alt West,
    Randall Yontz
Copy and Production Editors: Marsha Jahns,
    Nancy Nowiszewski, Mary Helen Schiltz, Carl Voss,
    David A. Walsh
Assistant Art Directors: Harijs Priekulis, Tom Wegner
Senior Graphic Designers: Alisann Dixon, Lynda Haupert,
    Lyne Neymeyer
Graphic Designers: Mike Burns, Mike Eagleton, Deb Miner,
    Stan Sams, D. Greg Thompson, Darla Whipple,
    Paul Zimmerman

Vice President, Editorial Director: Doris Eby
Group Editorial Services Director: Duane L. Gregg

General Manager: Fred Stines
Director of Publishing: Robert B. Nelson
Vice President, Retail Marketing: Jamie Martin
Vice President, Direct Marketing: Arthur Heydendael

## COOKING WITH WHOLE GRAINS

Editor: Diane Yanney
Copy and Production Editors: Nancy Nowiszewski, Carl Voss
Graphic Designer: Paul Zimmerman
Electronic Text Processor: Donna Russell

Contributing Photographer: Mike Dieter
Contributing Illustrator: Tom Rosborough

**On the cover:** *Grain Sprouts Braided Loaf* (see recipe, page 38).

# Contents

# Grains Identified

WHEAT

Cracked wheat

Wheat berries

Bulgur wheat

Whole wheat flour

Unprocessed wheat bran

Ready-to-cook couscous

Toasted wheat germ

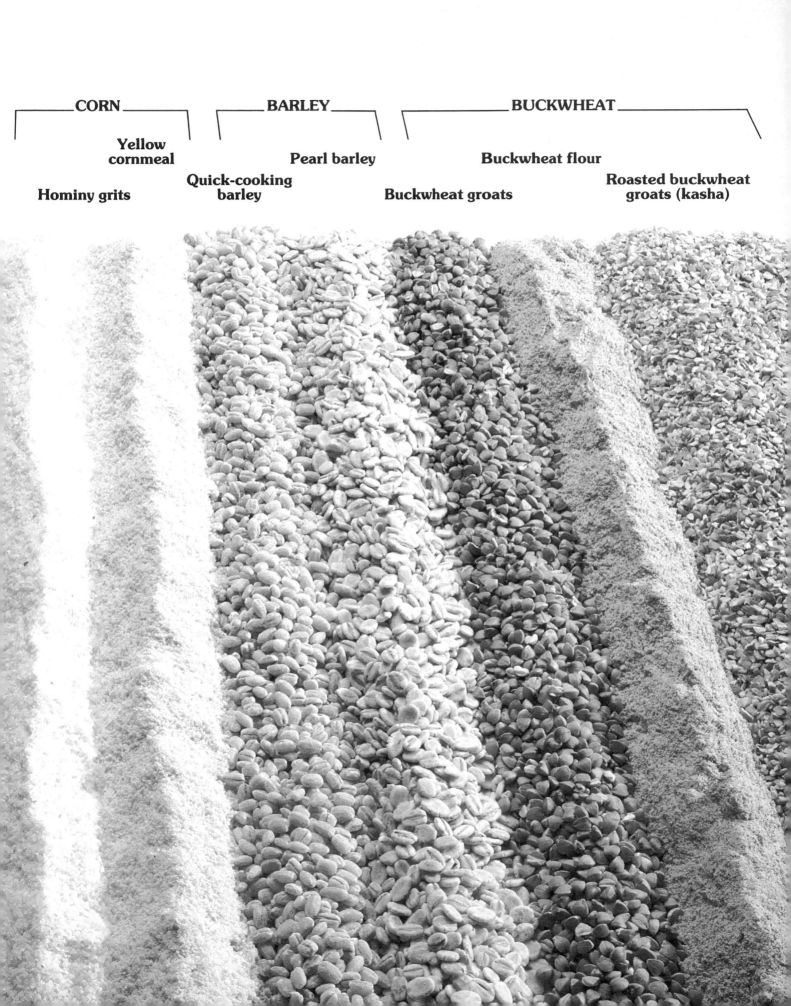

**CORN**

**BARLEY**

**BUCKWHEAT**

Yellow
cornmeal

Pearl barley

Buckwheat flour

Quick-cooking
barley

Roasted buckwheat
groats (kasha)

Hominy grits

Buckwheat groats

# Grains Identified

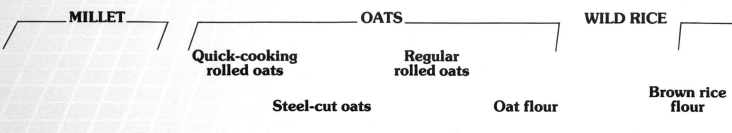

MILLET

OATS

WILD RICE

Quick-cooking rolled oats

Regular rolled oats

Steel-cut oats

Oat flour

Brown rice flour

BROWN
RICE

RYE

TRITICALE

Cracked rye

Rye berries

Triticale berries

Brown rice

Rye flour

Triticale flour

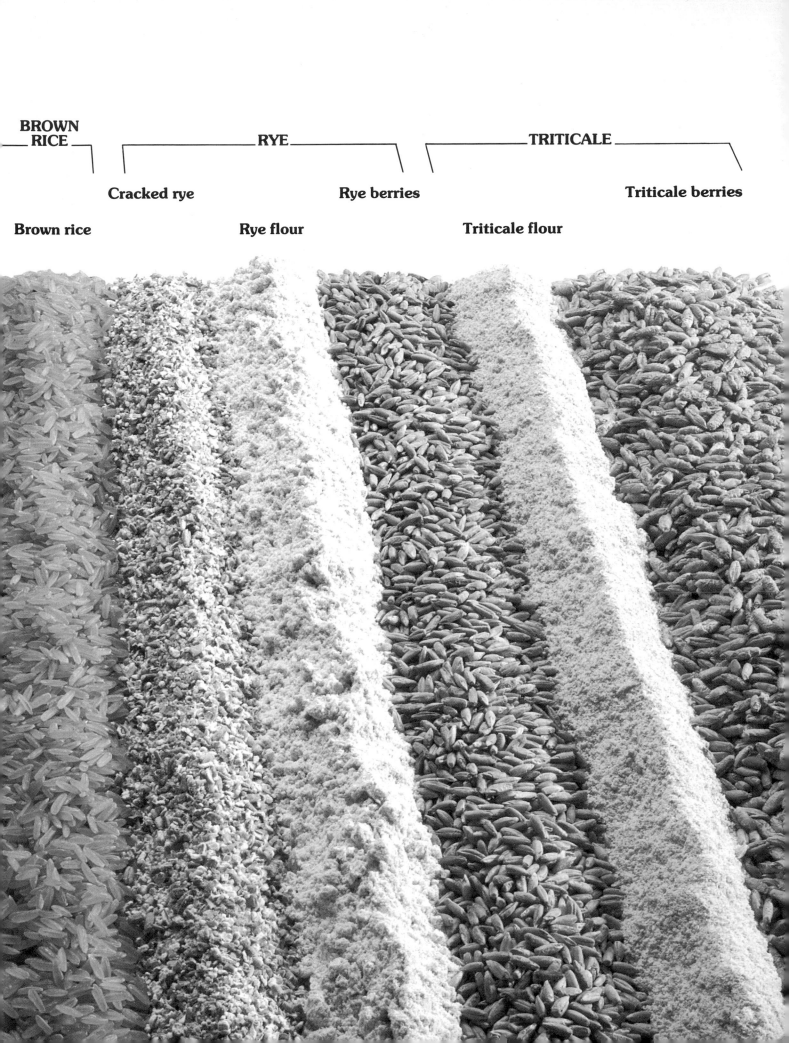

# Grain Cooking Basics

Use this chart as a guide for cooking grains. It's a handy reference when you can't put your hands on the package directions. Add 1 cup grain to the specified amount of boiling water. If desired, add ¼ to ½ teaspoon salt. Cook as directed.

*Note: For quick cooking of wheat, rye, or triticale berries, soak 1 cup berries in 3 cups water in the refrigerator overnight. Do not drain. Bring to boil; reduce heat. Simmer, covered, for 30 minutes.

| Grain Family | 1 Cup Grain | Boiling Water | Cooking Time | Yield |
|---|---|---|---|---|
| Wheat | *Wheat berries | 3 cups | Simmer, covered, for 1 hour. | 2½ cups |
| | Bulgur wheat | 2 cups | Simmer, covered, for 12 to 15 minutes. | 3 cups |
| | Cracked wheat | 2½ cups | Simmer, covered, for 15 to 20 minutes. Cover; let stand 5 minutes. | 2⅔ cups |
| | Ready-to-cook couscous | 1 cup | Cover with boiling water. Remove from heat; let stand 3 or 4 minutes. | 3 cups |
| Buckwheat | Buckwheat groats | 2½ cups | Simmer, covered, for 15 minutes. | 2⅔ cups |
| Oats | Regular rolled oats | 2 cups | Simmer, uncovered, for 5 to 8 minutes. Cover; let stand a few minutes. | 2 cups |
| | Quick-cooking rolled oats | 2 cups | Simmer, uncovered, for 1 minute. Cover; let stand 3 to 5 minutes. | 2 cups |
| | Steel-cut oats | 2½ cups | Simmer, covered, for 15 to 20 minutes. | 3 cups |
| Rye | Cracked rye | 2½ cups | Simmer, covered, for 10 to 15 minutes. Cover; let stand 5 minutes. | 2⅔ cups |
| | *Rye berries | 3 cups | Simmer, covered, for 1 hour. | 2½ cups |
| Millet | Millet | 3 cups | Simmer, covered, for 15 to 20 minutes. Cover; let stand 5 minutes. | 3½ cups |

| | | | | |
|---|---|---|---|---|
| Triticale | *Triticale berries | 3 cups | Simmer, covered, for 45 minutes. | 2 cups |
| Barley | Pearl barley | 4 cups | Simmer, covered, for 45 minutes. Drain. | 3½ cups |
| | Quick-cooking barley | 1½ cups | Simmer, covered, for 10 to 12 minutes. | 2½ cups |
| Corn | Cornmeal | 2¾ cups | Combine cornmeal and 1 cup cold water. Add to the boiling water. Simmer, covered, for 10 to 15 minutes. | 2 cups |
| | Quick-cooking hominy grits | 4 cups | Simmer, covered, for 5 to 6 minutes. | 2 cups |
| Wild Rice | Wild rice | 2 cups | Simmer, covered, for 40 to 50 minutes. | 3 cups |
| Rice | Brown rice | 2 cups | Simmer, covered, for 30 to 40 minutes. | 3 cups |

# Grains Glossary

**Barley:** Polished barley kernels; available in regular (pearl) and quick-cooking form.

**Brown rice:** Unpolished whole rice kernels; may be ground into rice flour.

**Buckwheat groats:** Whole, unpolished buckwheat kernels (roasted or unroasted); may be ground into buckwheat flour. Roasted kernels are called kasha.

**Bulgur wheat:** Precooked cracked wheat.

**Cornmeal:** Ground dried yellow or white corn kernels.

**Cracked rye:** Coarsely ground unpolished rye kernels.

**Cracked wheat:** Coarsely ground unpolished wheat kernels.

**Hominy grits:** Coarsely ground dried yellow or white corn kernels.

**Millet:** Unpolished yellow whole millet kernels.

**Quick-cooking rolled oats:** Cut, steamed, and flattened unpolished oat kernels; may be ground into oat flour.

**Ready-to-cook couscous:** Ground polished durum wheat kernels.

**Regular rolled oats:** Steamed and flattened unpolished oat kernels; may be ground into oat flour.

**Rye berries:** Whole rye kernels; may be ground into rye flour.

**Steel-cut oats:** Whole oat kernels cut into lengthwise pieces.

**Triticale berries:** Whole unpolished kernels—a cross between wheat and rye; may be ground into triticale flour.

**Unprocessed wheat bran:** Outer covering of the wheat kernel; also known as miller's bran.

**Wheat berries:** Unpolished whole wheat kernels; may be ground into whole wheat flour.

**Wheat germ:** Soft, oily portion of the wheat kernel.

**Wild rice:** Unpolished dark brown whole wild rice kernels; not a true member of the rice family.

# Wheat Cereal

| | | |
|---|---|---|
| **2 cups whole wheat flour**<br>**¼ cup toasted wheat germ**<br>**¾ teaspoon salt**<br>**⅔ cup water**<br>**½ cup creamy peanut butter** | ● Combine the 2 cups whole wheat flour, wheat germ, and salt. Stir water into peanut butter till smooth. Stir into flour mixture to make a moderately soft dough. Divide dough into fourths. | **Make this hearty cereal in special shapes using a pastry wheel or hors d'oeuvres cutters. Roll out dough as for flaked cereal and cut into desired shapes. Place on greased baking sheet. Bake and cool as directed, but *do not* break cereal.** |
| **Whole wheat flour** | ● Lightly sprinkle some whole wheat flour over a piece of waxed paper. Top with one portion of dough. Roll dough into a 12x9-inch rectangle. For flaked cereal, invert dough onto greased baking sheet. To make shaped cereal, see hint, right. Carefully peel off waxed paper. Repeat with remaining dough. | |
| **Milk *or* cream**<br>**Raisins *or* dates (optional)** | ● Bake in a 350° oven for 18 to 20 minutes or till lightly browned and crisp. Cool. Break into several large pieces. Place in plastic bag; break into small pieces with a rolling pin. Store in an airtight container. Serve with milk or cream and raisins or dates, if desired. Makes 3 cups. | |

# Bran Cereal

2 cups unprocessed wheat
    bran
1¼ cups water
½ cup nonfat dry milk
    powder
¼ cup cooking oil
1 tablespoon light molasses
1 teaspoon salt
2 cups whole wheat flour

● In a large bowl stir together the unprocessed wheat bran, the water, and the dry milk powder. Add the cooking oil, the molasses, and the salt. Mix well.

Stir in the 2 cups whole wheat flour. Form the dough into a ball. Divide the dough into fourths.

**Serve Bran Cereal anyway you like. Topped with cream or milk, it's a great morning starter—and it doesn't get soggy the way many commercial cereals do. Sprinkle with raisins, dates, or figs for a change of taste.**

**Or, crush this crunchy concoction for an easy ice cream topper.**

**Whole wheat flour**

● Lightly sprinkle some whole wheat flour over a piece of waxed paper. Top with one portion of dough. Roll dough into a 14x10-inch rectangle. For flaked cereal, invert dough onto a greased baking sheet. To make shaped cereal, see hint on opposite page. Carefully peel off the waxed paper. Repeat with the remaining dough.

**Milk *or* cream**

● Bake in a 375° oven for 20 to 25 minutes or till lightly browned and crisp. Cool. Break into several large pieces. Place in a plastic bag; break into small pieces with a rolling pin. Store in an airtight container. Serve with milk or cream. Makes about 5 cups.

# Fruity Breakfast Barley

1¼ **cups water**
1 **cup orange juice**
¼ **cup snipped dried apricots**
   **Dash ground cloves**
1 **cup quick-cooking barley**
1 **tablespoon butter *or* margarine**
¼ **cup chopped nuts (optional)**
   **Milk *or* cream (optional)**

● In medium saucepan combine water, orange juice, apricots, and cloves. Bring to boiling. Add barley. Simmer, covered, for 12 to 15 minutes or till barley is tender. Stir in butter or margarine. Turn into serving bowls; sprinkle with nuts, if desired. Serve with milk or cream, if desired. Makes 4 servings.

**Start the day with a breakfast surprise—put this flavorful and filling barley cereal on the table. Once you taste this fruity combination, you won't think of barley as "just for soups" again.**

# Good-for-You Granola

3 **cups rolled oats**
1 **cup coconut**
1 **cup sliced almonds**
½ **cup toasted wheat germ**
½ **cup sesame seed**
⅓ **cup maple syrup *or* maple-flavored syrup**
⅓ **cup butter *or* margarine, melted**

● Stir together the rolled oats, the coconut, the sliced almonds, the toasted wheat germ, and the sesame seed. Stir in maple syrup and butter or margarine. Spread in a 15x10x1-inch baking pan. Bake in a 375° oven for 15 to 20 minutes, stirring once.

1 **cup raisins**
   **Milk *or* cream (optional)**

● Stir in raisins. Cool. Store in an airtight container in a cool, dry place or in the refrigerator. Serve with milk or light cream. Makes about 7 cups.

**You can't beat homemade granola for good taste. Serve it with cream or milk for a breakfast pick-me-up. Or pack some in plastic bags or containers as a take-along snack.**

   **For a real treat, use this mix to make a batch of Chewy Granola Bars (see recipe, page 81). We guarantee you'll like them better than the store-bought kind.**

# Wheat Berry-Orange Cereal

2 **cups cooked wheat, rye, *or* triticale berries (see cooking directions, pages 8 and 9)**
½ **cup orange juice *or* unsweetened pineapple juice**
1 **tablespoon brown sugar**
¼ **teaspoon salt**
½ **cup toasted coconut**
½ **teaspoon finely shredded orange peel**
   **Milk *or* cream (optional)**

● In saucepan combine cooked wheat, rye, or triticale berries, orange juice or pineapple juice, brown sugar, and salt. Bring to boiling. Reduce heat; simmer, covered, for 10 minutes.
   Stir in toasted coconut and finely shredded orange peel. Heat through.
   Serve with milk or cream, if desired. Makes 4 servings.

**Did you make too much cereal? Don't throw it away—warming leftovers is easy. In a saucepan cook ½ cup cooked cereal with 1 tablespoon *water* over low heat for 5 minutes. Or, put ½ cup cooked cereal into a bowl; cover with waxed paper. Micro-cook on HIGH for 45 seconds.**

# Mixed Grain Cereal

| | |
|---|---|
| 1 **cup regular rolled oats**<br>1 **cup quick-cooking barley**<br>1 **cup cracked wheat**<br>1 **cup sunflower nuts**<br>1 **cup raisins (optional)**<br>½ **cup millet** | ● Combine regular rolled oats; quick-cooking barley; cracked wheat; sunflower nuts; raisins, if desired, and millet in airtight storage container. Makes 5½ cups mix. |
| 1⅓ **cups water**<br>**Milk** *or* **cream**<br>**Honey** *or* **brown sugar** | ● **To make 4 servings:** In saucepan bring water to boiling. Stir in *¾ cup* of the cereal mixture. Simmer, covered, for 12 to 15 minutes or to desired consistency. Serve with milk or cream and honey or brown sugar. |

**When it's time to replenish your supply of hot cereal mixes, add Mixed Grain Cereal to the shelf. It's so quick to make. And so easy to like.**

# Two-Grain Cereal

| | |
|---|---|
| 1 **cup cornmeal**<br>1 **cup ready-to-cook**<br>   **couscous**<br>½ **cup snipped dried apple**<br>½ **cup dried currants**<br>½ **teaspoon ground nutmeg**<br>½ **teaspoon ground**<br>   **cinnamon** | ● Combine the cornmeal, ready-to-cook couscous, snipped dried apple, dried currants, ground nutmeg, and ground cinnamon in an airtight storage container. Makes about 3 cups mix. |
| 2 **cups water**<br>¼ **teaspoon salt**<br>**Milk** *or* **cream** | ● **To make 3 servings:** In saucepan bring water and salt to boiling. Slowly stir in *½ cup* of the cereal mixture. Simmer, uncovered, for 10 to 15 minutes or to desired consistency. Serve with milk or cream. |

**Couscous is a traditional North African side dish normally served with spicy meat and vegetable combinations. But we've used this fine-grained product for a top-of-the-morning treat. Its texture and appearance will remind you of farina.**

# Oatmeal-Applesauce Doughnuts

| | |
|---|---|
| 2 cups all-purpose flour<br>1 cup rolled oats<br>2 teaspoons baking powder<br>½ teaspoon salt<br>½ teaspoon ground cinnamon<br>½ teaspoon ground nutmeg | ● In a mixing bowl stir together the flour, the rolled oats, the baking powder, the salt, the ground cinnamon, and the ground nutmeg; set aside. |
| 2 beaten eggs<br>½ cup packed brown sugar<br>½ cup applesauce<br>¼ cup butter *or* margarine, melted | ● In a small mixing bowl stir together eggs, brown sugar, applesauce, and butter. Add *egg* mixture all at once to flour mixture, stirring just till blended. Cover; chill dough about 2 hours. |
| Cooking oil for deep-fat frying | ● Turn dough out onto lightly floured surface. Roll into a 9-inch circle or about ⅝ inch thick. Cut with floured 2½-inch doughnut cutter. Fry doughnuts, a few at a time, in deep, hot fat (365°) about 1 minute per side or till golden brown. Drain on paper toweling. |
| 1½ cups sifted powdered sugar<br>½ teaspoon vanilla<br>2 to 3 tablespoons milk | ● For glaze, in a small bowl combine the powdered sugar and vanilla. Stir in enough milk to make glaze of drizzling consistency. Dip warm doughnuts in glaze. Let dry on wire rack. Makes 8 to 10 doughnuts. |

You can make doughnuts even if you don't own a deep-fat fryer. A deep, heavy saucepan will work just as well.

And don't forget to use a deep-fat frying thermometer. The correct temperature is a must for perfect fried foods. If the temperature is too high, the food will burn, but not be cooked through. At too low a temperature, fried foods will be greasy.

Save the cooking oil you used for frying for another day. When the oil has cooled completely, strain it through cheesecloth. Then store the oil, covered, in the refrigerator.

# Rye-Raisin Fritters

1 cup rye flour
2 tablespoons brown sugar
1 tablespoon baking powder
½ teaspoon ground cinnamon
¼ teaspoon salt

● In a mixing bowl stir together the rye flour, brown sugar, baking powder, cinnamon, and salt; set aside.

1 beaten egg
¼ cup milk
1 tablespoon cooking oil
½ cup raisins

● Stir together the egg, the milk, and the 1 tablespoon cooking oil. Stir in the raisins. Add the milk mixture to the flour mixture, stirring just till moistened; do not beat smooth.

Cooking oil for deep-fat frying

● Drop batter by tablespoonfuls into deep, hot fat (375°). Fry 4 or 5 fritters at a time, about 2 minutes per side or till done. Drain on paper toweling.

Maple-flavored syrup *or* powdered sugar

● Serve hot with syrup or dust with powdered sugar. Makes 12 to 14 fritters.

# Apple-Grain Coffee Cake

²⁄₃ cup sugar
¹⁄₃ cup butter *or* margarine
1 egg
¹⁄₂ cup apple juice
¹⁄₂ cup coarsely shredded peeled apple

● In a small mixer bowl beat together the sugar and butter or margarine. Beat in egg. Add apple juice and ¹⁄₂ cup coarsely shredded apple.

**Cut cored and peeled apples into thirds. Slice each third into 5 slices. Brush with lemon juice.**

³⁄₄ cup all-purpose flour
¹⁄₂ cup whole wheat flour
1 teaspoon baking powder
1 teaspoon ground cinnamon
¹⁄₂ teaspoon baking soda
¹⁄₄ teaspoon ground allspice
1¹⁄₂ cups quick-cooking rolled oats

● Stir together the all-purpose flour, whole wheat flour, baking powder, cinnamon, baking soda, and allspice. Add to beaten mixture; mix well.
   Fold in the quick-cooking rolled oats. Pour into a well-greased 9x1¹⁄₂-inch round baking pan.

2 medium cooking apples, peeled and cored
Lemon juice

● Cut the 2 apples into thirds lengthwise. Slice each third into 5 slices. Keeping slices together, brush them with lemon juice, and place each group of slices in batter at about 2-inch intervals, forming a circle. Bake in a 375° oven for 40 to 45 minutes or till done.

**Keeping slices together, place groups of 5 slices at about 2-inch intervals, forming a circle in the coffee-cake batter.**

¹⁄₃ cup apple jelly

● In small saucepan over low heat melt apple jelly. Brush jelly atop warm coffee cake. Allow coffee cake to cool on wire rack 10 minutes before serving. Serve warm or cool. Makes 10 to 12 servings.

# Wheat Berry Popovers

| 1 cup water<br>2 tablespoons wheat berries | ● In saucepan combine water and wheat berries. Bring to boiling. Reduce heat; simmer, covered, for 1 hour or till berries are tender but still chewy. Drain, cool, and finely chop the wheat berries. |
| --- | --- |
| 1½ teaspoons shortening | ● Grease six 6-ounce custard cups, using ¼ teaspoon shortening for each. Or, grease 10 muffin cups. Place on a 15x10x1-inch baking pan. Heat in a 450° oven for 5 minutes. |
| 3 eggs<br>1½ cups milk<br>1 tablespoon cooking oil<br>½ cup all-purpose flour<br>½ cup whole wheat flour<br>½ teaspoon salt | ● Combine eggs, milk, and oil; add all-purpose flour, whole wheat flour, and salt. Beat with electric mixer or rotary beater till smooth. Stir in the chopped wheat berries.<br>　Fill hot custard cups or muffin cups about ¾ full. Bake in a 450° oven for 20 minutes. Reduce oven temperature to 350° and bake 15 to 20 minutes more or till popovers are very firm. A few minutes before removing from oven, prick each popover with a fork to let steam escape. Serve hot.<br>　For crisper popovers, turn off oven and leave popovers in the oven 10 minutes longer. Makes 6 or 10 popovers. |

**Don't peek at the popovers until they've baked at least 15 minutes. If you open the oven door sooner, you let in cool air. Cool air condenses the steam inside the popovers and causes them to collapse.**

# Savory Rice Flour Waffles

|  |  |
|---|---|
| 1 cup brown rice flour (see tip, opposite)<br>½ cup all-purpose flour<br>2 slices bacon, crisp-cooked, drained, and crumbled<br>1 tablespoon baking powder<br>½ teaspoon paprika<br>⅛ teaspoon salt | ● In large mixing bowl stir together the brown rice flour, all-purpose flour, crisp-cooked and crumbled bacon, baking powder, paprika, and salt. |
| 2 egg yolks<br>1 8-ounce carton dairy sour cream<br>¾ cup milk<br>¼ cup cooking oil *or* shortening, melted | ● In small mixing bowl beat egg yolks with fork. Beat in sour cream, milk, and cooking oil or shortening. Add to flour mixture all at once. Stir mixture till blended but still slightly lumpy. |
| 2 egg whites | ● In small mixer bowl beat egg whites till stiff peaks form. Gently fold egg whites into egg yolk mixture, leaving a few fluffs of egg white. *Do not* overmix. |
| | ● Carefully pour batter into grids of preheated, lightly greased waffle baker. Close lid quickly; do not open during baking. Use a fork to help lift the baked waffle off grid.<br>   To keep baked waffles hot for serving, place in single layer on wire rack placed atop a baking sheet in warm oven. Makes three (9-inch) waffles. |

**Brown rice flour makes these waffles tender and a little bit crunchy. Grinding your own flour is easy (see tip, opposite)— especially for small amounts of flour. But if you'd rather, you can buy brown rice flour in health food stores.**

# Oat Coffee Ring

| | |
|---|---|
| ⅓ cup shortening<br>¾ cup packed brown sugar<br>2 eggs | ● In a mixer bowl beat shortening on medium speed of an electric mixer for 30 seconds. Add sugar and beat till fluffy. Add eggs; beat well. |
| 1 cup all-purpose flour<br>½ cup oat flour (see tip, below)<br>1½ teaspoons baking powder<br>½ teaspoon baking soda<br>½ teaspoon salt | ● In a mixing bowl stir together the all-purpose flour, the oat flour, the baking powder, the baking soda, and the salt. |
| ½ cup buttermilk *or* sour milk | ● Add flour mixture and buttermilk alternately to sugar mixture. Beat just till smooth after each addition. |
| 2 tablespoons rolled oats | ● Sprinkle oats on bottom and sides of a greased 8-inch fluted tube pan or a 6½-cup ring mold. Spoon batter into prepared pan. Bake in a 350° oven for 35 to 45 minutes. Cool in pan 10 minutes on wire rack; turn out onto platter. Serve warm. Makes 1 ring. |

**This coffee bread is so light and tender you'll think you're eating cake. If you want to make it ahead, cool the ring completely. Then wrap it in foil and store it at room temperature for up to 24 hours. Before serving, reheat the ring in a 350° oven for 15 minutes.**

# Grinding Grains

Convert whole grain kernels to flour in no time by using your blender as a grain grinder. Only blenders with glass blending containers are recommended since grains will scratch plastic containers. Grind 1 cup of grain at a time, using the highest speed or "grind" setting. (Brown rice is an exception: only grind ½ cup at a time.) Be sure the blender lid is securely in place before you start. It takes about 3 minutes to grind 1 cup of wheat, rye, or triticale berries, about 1½ to 2 minutes for ½ cup of brown rice, and about 1 minute for 1 cup of rolled oats.

# Wheat Germ Corn Muffins

| | |
|---|---|
| 1 | cup all-purpose flour |
| ½ | cup toasted wheat germ |
| ½ | cup cornmeal |
| 2 | tablespoons sugar |
| 1 | tablespoon baking powder |
| ½ | teaspoon salt |

● In a large mixing bowl stir together the all-purpose flour, the toasted wheat germ, the cornmeal, the sugar, the baking powder, and the salt. Make a well in the center.

| | |
|---|---|
| 1 | beaten egg |
| 1 | cup milk |
| ¼ | cup butter *or* margarine, melted |

● Combine egg, milk, and melted butter or margarine; add all at once to flour mixture. Stir just till moistened; batter should be lumpy. Grease muffin pan or line with paper bake cups; fill ⅔ full.
  Bake in a 400° oven for 20 minutes or till muffins are lightly browned. Serve warm. Makes 12 muffins.

**Save leftover muffins for later. To freeze extras, wrap muffins in moisture-vaporproof material. Seal, label, and freeze for up to 2 months. To serve, pop unwrapped muffins in a 300° oven for 25 minutes or till heated through.**

# Spicy Apple-Kasha Muffins

| | |
|---|---|
| 1 | cup apple cider *or* juice |
| ¾ | cup finely ground roasted buckwheat groats (kasha) |

● In a mixing bowl pour the apple cider or the apple juice over the buckwheat groats. Let stand 5 minutes.

| | |
|---|---|
| 1 | egg |
| ¼ | cup cooking oil |
| 1½ | cups all-purpose flour |
| ⅓ | cup packed brown sugar |
| 2 | teaspoons baking powder |
| ½ | teaspoon baking soda |
| ½ | teaspoon salt |
| ½ | teaspoon ground cinnamon |
| ½ | teaspoon ground ginger |
| 1 | cup finely chopped, peeled apple |

● Add egg and cooking oil to groats; mix well. Stir together flour, brown sugar, baking powder, baking soda, salt, cinnamon, and ginger. Add to buckwheat mixture, stirring just till moistened. Fold in finely chopped apple.
  Grease muffin pan or line with paper bake cups; fill ⅔ full. Bake in a 400° oven for 20 to 25 minutes. Serve warm. Makes 12 to 15 muffins.

**If you can't find ground roasted buckwheat groats in your grocery store, ask for kasha—its commonly used name. Check the package label before buying. Kasha is available in fine, medium, and coarse grinds.**

# Refrigerator Bran Muffin Mix

1½ cups all-purpose flour
 1 cup unprocessed wheat bran
 2 teaspoons baking powder
 1 teaspoon ground cinnamon
 ½ teaspoon salt
 ¼ teaspoon ground nutmeg

● In a mixing bowl stir together the all-purpose flour, the unprocessed wheat bran, the baking powder, the ground cinnamon, the salt, and the ground nutmeg. Make a well in the center.

 2 beaten eggs
 ¾ cup milk
 ⅓ cup packed brown sugar
 ¼ cup cooking oil *or* melted shortening
 1 teaspoon finely shredded orange peel
 ⅓ cup chopped nuts

● Combine eggs, milk, brown sugar, cooking oil, and orange peel. Add egg mixture to flour mixture; stir just till moistened. Fold in nuts. Store in covered container in refrigerator up to 10 days.

To bake, stir batter. Grease muffin pans or line with paper bake cups; fill ⅔ full. Bake in a 400° oven for 15 to 20 minutes. Serve warm. Makes 12 muffins.

**Want just one or two bran muffins? Cook them fast in a microwave oven. Line one or two 6-ounce custard cups with a paper bake cup. Spoon about 2 tablespoons batter into each. For one muffin, micro-cook on HIGH for 35 seconds; for two muffins, micro-cook on HIGH for 50 seconds.**

# Crunchy Corn Bread

| | | |
|---|---|---|
| 1 cup boiling water<br>¼ cup cracked wheat *or* bulgur wheat | ● Pour the water over the cracked wheat or the bulgur wheat. Let stand for 5 minutes; drain. | **Add Crunchy Corn Bread to your list of breakfast specials. It's a refreshing change from pancakes, cold cereal, or toast. Serve it piping hot from the oven. That's the best way to get the subtle sweetness of the maple syrup drizzle.** |
| 1 cup all-purpose flour<br>1 cup yellow cornmeal<br>½ cup quick-cooking rolled oats<br>¼ cup sugar<br>4 teaspoons baking powder<br>½ teaspoon salt | ● In a mixing bowl stir together the all-purpose flour, the yellow cornmeal, the quick-cooking rolled oats, the sugar, the baking powder, and the salt. | |
| 2 slightly beaten eggs<br>⅔ cup milk | ● Add cracked wheat, eggs, and milk; stir till mixture is moistened. | |
| ½ cup chopped pecans<br>2 tablespoons maple-flavored syrup | ● Stir in pecans. Spread batter evenly in a greased 9x9x2-inch baking pan. Drizzle with the 2 tablespoons maple-flavored syrup. Bake in a 400° oven about 20 minutes or till done. | |
| Maple-flavored syrup, butter, *or* margarine | ● Serve warm cut into squares with additional maple-flavored syrup, butter, or margarine. Makes 9 servings. | |

# Wheat and Cheese Spirals

| | |
|---|---|
| 2 cups whole wheat flour<br>2 teaspoons baking powder<br>¼ teaspoon salt | ● In a mixing bowl stir together the whole wheat flour, the baking powder, and the salt. |
| ½ cup butter *or* margarine | ● Cut in ½ cup butter or margarine till mixture resembles coarse crumbs. |
| 1 beaten egg<br>⅔ cup milk | ● Make a well in the center. Combine egg and milk; add all at once to dry ingredients. Stir just till dough clings together. Knead gently on a lightly floured surface for 12 to 15 strokes. Roll dough into a 15x6-inch rectangle. |
| ½ cup shredded Monterey Jack cheese with jalapeño peppers<br>Melted butter *or* margarine<br>Sesame seed, poppy seed, toasted wheat germ, *or* dillseed | ● Sprinkle cheese over dough. Fold dough in half lengthwise to make a 15x3-inch rectangle. Cut into fifteen 3x1-inch strips. Holding a strip at both ends, twist in opposite directions twice to form a spiral.<br>    Place on lightly greased baking sheet, pressing both ends down. Brush with melted butter; sprinkle with sesame seed, poppy seed, toasted wheat germ, or dillseed. Bake in a 450° oven for 8 to 10 minutes. Serve warm. Makes 15 spirals. |

**Monterey Jack cheese with jalapeño peppers adds a little zing to Wheat and Cheese Spirals. You may be fooled when you bite into them. They have the tender texture of yeast breads, but are actually made like biscuits. Serve them with soups or salads. On their own, they're great as snacks.**

# Bacon-Cornmeal Pancakes

| | |
|---|---|
| 1 | cup all-purpose flour |
| ¾ | cup cornmeal |
| 1 | tablespoon sugar |
| 2 | teaspoons baking powder |

● In mixing bowl combine flour, cornmeal, sugar, and baking powder.

| | |
|---|---|
| 2 | beaten eggs |
| 1½ | cups milk |
| 1 | tablespoon cooking oil |
| 4 | slices bacon, crisp-cooked, drained, and crumbled |
| | Maple-flavored syrup (optional) |

● Combine eggs, milk, and oil; add all at once to dry ingredients. Stir in bacon.

For each pancake, pour ¼ *cup* batter onto hot, lightly greased griddle or heavy skillet. Cook till golden brown, turning to cook on other side when pancake has a bubbly surface and slightly dry edges.

Serve with maple-flavored syrup, if desired. Makes twelve (4-inch) pancakes.

**Today we call these hearty cornmeal favorites pancakes because that's how we serve them. But colonial cooks called them johnnycakes and used them more like bread. We've added crisp bacon bits to this early American favorite to appeal to contemporary pancake fans.**

**Cinnamon-Buckwheat Pancakes (see recipe, page 27)**

# Whole Wheat-Buttermilk Flapjacks

| | |
|---|---|
| 1 | cup whole wheat flour |
| ¼ | cup all-purpose flour |
| 2 | tablespoons toasted wheat germ |
| 1 | tablespoon brown sugar |
| 1 | teaspoon baking powder |
| ½ | teaspoon salt |
| ¼ | teaspoon baking soda |

● In mixing bowl stir together the whole wheat flour, the all-purpose flour, the wheat germ, the brown sugar, the baking powder, the salt, and the baking soda.

| | |
|---|---|
| 1 | beaten egg |
| 1¼ | cups buttermilk *or* sour milk |
| 1 | tablespoon cooking oil |
| | Maple-flavored syrup *and/or* fresh fruit (optional) |

● Combine the egg, the buttermilk, and the oil. Add egg mixture to flour mixture all at once. Stir till blended.

For each pancake, pour about *¼ cup* batter onto a hot, lightly greased griddle or into a heavy skillet. Cook over medium heat till golden brown, turning to cook other side when pancake has a bubbly surface and slightly dry edges.

Serve pancakes with maple-flavored syrup and/or fresh fruit, if desired. Makes eight (4-inch) pancakes.

**Perfect pancakes require griddle know-how. Start by heating a griddle or heavy skillet over medium heat. Sprinkle a few drops of water on the griddle. When the drops dance across the surface, it's time to add the pancake batter. Don't forget to leave room for the pancakes to expand as they cook so they won't run together.**

**Whole Wheat-Buttermilk Flapjacks**

# Oatmeal Pancakes

| | |
|---|---|
| 1 cup milk<br>¾ cup quick-cooking rolled oats | ● In a small saucepan heat milk till hot. Stir in oats; let stand for 5 minutes. |
| ¾ cup oat flour (see tip, page 19)<br>2 tablespoons sugar<br>2 teaspoons baking powder<br>½ teaspoon salt | ● In mixing bowl combine oat flour, sugar, baking powder, and salt. Add oat-milk mixture. |
| 2 beaten egg yolks<br>1 tablespoon cooking oil | ● Combine egg yolks and cooking oil; add all at once to flour-oat mixture, stirring just till combined. |
| 2 egg whites | ● Beat egg whites till stiff peaks form; fold into the batter. For each pancake, pour about ¼ *cup* of the batter onto hot, lightly greased griddle or heavy skillet. Cook till golden brown, turning to cook other side when pancake has a bubbly surface and slightly dry edges. |
| Maple-flavored syrup (optional) | ● Serve pancakes with maple-flavored syrup, if desired. Makes about eight (4-inch) pancakes. |

**Use a ¼-cup measure as a handy scoop for transferring pancake batter from the bowl to the griddle. If you want smaller pancakes, switch to a 1-tablespoon measure. That will put just the right amount of batter on the griddle for dollar-size pancakes.**

# Cinnamon Buckwheat Pancakes

*Pictured on page 24—*

¾ cup all-purpose flour
½ cup buckwheat flour
2 teaspoons baking powder
½ teaspoon salt
¼ teaspoon ground
  cinnamon

● In mixing bowl combine all-purpose flour, buckwheat flour, baking powder, salt, and cinnamon.

1 beaten egg
1 cup milk
2 tablespoons maple-
  flavored syrup *or* honey
1 tablespoon cooking oil
  Maple-flavored syrup
  *and/or* fresh fruit
  (optional)

● Stir together the egg, milk, syrup, and oil. Add all at once to flour mixture, stirring just till combined. For each pancake, pour about ¼ *cup* batter onto hot, lightly greased griddle or heavy skillet. Cook till golden brown, turning to cook other side when pancake has a bubbly surface and slightly dry edges. Serve pancakes with maple-flavored syrup and/or fresh fruit, if desired. Makes about eight (4-inch) pancakes.

**Applesauce-Cinnamon Buckwheat Pancakes:** Prepare Cinnamon Buckwheat Pancakes as directed above, *except* decrease milk to ⅔ cup and add ½ cup *applesauce* to egg mixture.

**To many folks the flavor of buckwheat may be unfamiliar and, at first bite, seem unusual. But these wholesome pancakes, with their subtle flavor and touch of cinnamon, are sure to make buckwheat a favorite breakfast treat.**

# Pancakes Plus

Perk up plain pancakes with added nuts or fruit. Use ½ cup chopped nuts, chopped apple, or well-drained blueberries for recipes that yield about 8 pancakes. Prepare pancakes as directed (see recipes, pages 24-27), *except* sprinkle each pancake with about 1 tablespoon nuts, apples, or berries before turning.

# Bread-Making Basics

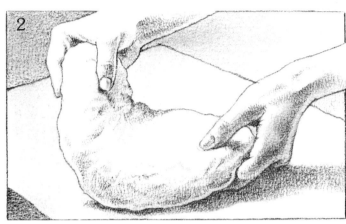

**1** To knead bread dough, turn the dough out onto a lightly floured surface or a well-floured pastry cloth. Fold the bread dough over and push it down with the heels of your hands, curving your fingers over the dough.

**2** Give the dough a quarter turn, then fold over and push down again. Kneading is important in determining the final structure of the loaf. If the dough is not kneaded enough, the loaf will have a coarse texture and will not rise as high. Continue kneading until the dough is smooth and elastic. To be sure you've kneaded enough, set a timer for the time suggested in the recipe. You may want to stop and rest instead of kneading the dough all at once. Just be sure that the total kneading time is as long as the recipe suggests.

**3** Shape the dough into a ball. Place it into a large greased bowl and turn it over once to grease the surface. Cover the bowl with a cloth. Let dough rise in a warm place till double (1 to 1½ hours). The oven is a good draft-free place to set the dough. Place the bowl of dough on the upper rack with a pan of hot water on the lower rack. Close door.

**4** The dough should be allowed to rise till it doubles in size. The times suggested in the yeast bread recipes are guidelines. The actual rising time needed may be more or less. The dough is ready to shape when you can lightly press 2 fingertips ½ inch into the dough and the indentations remain.

# Bread-Making Basics

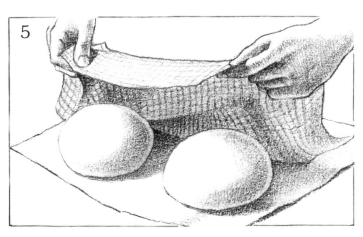

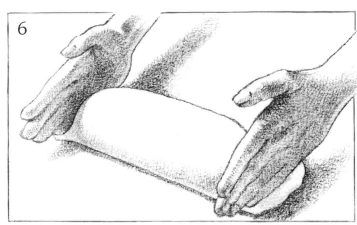

**5** Punch down the dough by pushing your fist into the center of the dough. Then pull the edges to the center, turn dough over, and place on a lightly floured surface or a well-floured pastry cloth. Divide the dough in half (or according to recipe directions). Shape into smooth balls. Cover; let the dough rest for 10 minutes.

**6** Roll the dough into a 12x8-inch rectangle. Roll up tightly, starting from the narrow edge. Seal the ends by pressing down on each end to make a thin strip. Fold strips under. Place loaf in a greased 8x4x2-inch loaf pan. Repeat for second loaf.

**7** Cover the loaves; let rise in warm place till double (about 35 minutes). Lightly touch the loaf with your index finger. It is ready to bake when an indentation remains.

**8** Bake bread as directed in recipe. Tap the top. A hollow sound means the loaf is done. If the top browns too fast, cover with foil the last 15 minutes of baking.

# Add-a-Grain Bread

2¼ to 3¾ cups whole wheat flour
2 packages active dry yeast

● In large mixer bowl combine *2 cups* of the whole wheat flour and the yeast.

There's no limit to the variety of bread loaves you can bake using this basic recipe. It's a good way to use leftover grains or try new grains. You can substitute whole grains for all or only part of the 3 cups all-purpose flour.

1¾ cups milk
⅓ cup honey *or* molasses
3 tablespoons butter, margarine, *or* cooking oil
2 teaspoons salt

● Heat milk, honey, butter, and salt just till warm (115° to 120°) and butter is almost melted; stir constantly. Add to flour mixture. Beat at low speed of electric mixer ½ minute, scraping bowl. Beat 3 minutes at high speed.

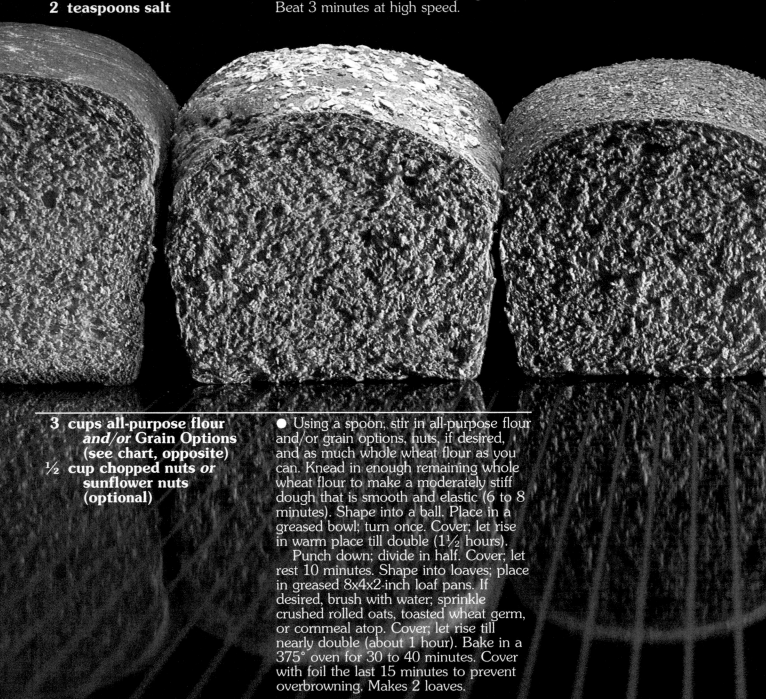

3 cups all-purpose flour *and/or* Grain Options (see chart, opposite)
½ cup chopped nuts *or* sunflower nuts (optional)

● Using a spoon, stir in all-purpose flour and/or grain options, nuts, if desired, and as much whole wheat flour as you can. Knead in enough remaining whole wheat flour to make a moderately stiff dough that is smooth and elastic (6 to 8 minutes). Shape into a ball. Place in a greased bowl; turn once. Cover; let rise in warm place till double (1½ hours).

Punch down; divide in half. Cover; let rest 10 minutes. Shape into loaves; place in greased 8x4x2-inch loaf pans. If desired, brush with water; sprinkle crushed rolled oats, toasted wheat germ, or cornmeal atop. Cover; let rise till nearly double (about 1 hour). Bake in a 375° oven for 30 to 40 minutes. Cover with foil the last 15 minutes to prevent overbrowning. Makes 2 loaves.

# Grain Options

| Grain | Maximum Amount | Notes | |
|---|---|---|---|
| Whole wheat flour<br>Rye flour | 3 cups | | Use any combination of these grains or a combination of these grains and all-purpose flour to equal 3 cups. The less all-purpose flour you use the heavier and coarser your bread will be. |
| Quick-cooking rolled oats<br>Regular rolled oats | 2 cups | | |
| Buckwheat flour<br>Triticale flour | 1 cup | | |
| Unprocessed wheat bran<br>Cornmeal | 1 cup | | |
| Toasted wheat germ | ½ cup | | |
| Cracked wheat<br>Cracked rye<br>Steel-cut oats<br>Bulgur wheat<br>Buckwheat groats<br>Millet | ½ cup | In saucepan combine grain and 1 cup *boiling water*. Let stand, covered, for 5 minutes. Drain well. | |

# Cracked Wheat Italian Bread

| | | |
|---|---|---|
| **4½ to 5 cups all-purpose flour**<br>**2 packages active dry yeast** | ● In a large mixer bowl combine *2 cups* of the flour and the yeast. | **Look for cracked wheat in a health foods store or in the specialty section of your grocery store. If it's not available, you can grind whole wheat kernels (wheat berries) in your blender. Just follow the tip for grinding grains (see page 19), *except* grind for half of the time suggested to produce flour. Cracked wheat adds lots of whole grain texture to this bread, so keep the grains somewhat coarse.** |
| **2 cups warm water (115° to 120°)**<br>**2 tablespoons cooking oil**<br>**1 tablespoon molasses**<br>**2 teaspoons salt** | ● Combine water, oil, molasses, and salt; add to flour mixture. Beat at low speed of electric mixer for 30 seconds, scraping sides of bowl constantly. Beat 3 minutes at high speed. | |
| **1½ cups cracked wheat** | ● Stir in cracked wheat till well combined. Using a spoon, stir in as much remaining flour as you can. On lightly floured surface knead in enough remaining flour to make a moderately stiff dough that is smooth and elastic (6 to 8 minutes). Place dough in a lightly greased bowl; turn once to grease surface. Cover and let rise in a warm place till double (1 to 1¼ hours). | |
| | ● Punch down. For large loaves, divide dough in half. Cover and let stand 10 minutes. Shape into 2 loaves about 15 inches long, tapering the ends. For individual loaves, divide dough into 16 pieces; shape into balls. Cover and let stand 10 minutes. Shape each ball into a 6-inch loaf; taper the ends. | |
| **Cornmeal**<br>**Milk** | ● Place on a greased baking sheet sprinkled with cornmeal. Cover and let rise till nearly double (about 45 minutes). With sharp knife, make 3 or 4 diagonal slashes about ¼ inch deep across tops of large loaves and 2 or 3 shallow cuts across tops of individual loaves. Brush loaves with milk. Bake large loaves in a 375° oven for 35 to 40 minutes. Bake individual loaves for 25 to 30 minutes. Remove from baking sheet. Cool on wire rack. Makes 2 large loaves or 16 individual loaves. | |

# Swiss Rye Bread

| | |
|---|---|
| 1½ to 1¾ cups all-purpose flour<br>1 package active dry yeast | ● In a large mixer bowl combine *1 cup* of the flour and the yeast. |
| 1 cup milk<br>1 tablespoon sugar<br>¾ teaspoon salt<br>¾ cup shredded Swiss *or* cheddar cheese (3 ounces) | ● In saucepan heat milk, sugar, and salt just till warm (115° to 120°); stir constantly. Add to flour mixture; add cheese. Beat at low speed of electric mixer ½ minute, scraping sides of bowl constantly. Beat 3 minutes at high speed. |
| ¾ cup rye flour *or* triticale flour | ● Using a spoon, stir in rye or triticale flour and as much of the remaining all-purpose flour as you can. Turn out onto lightly floured surface. Knead in enough of the remaining all-purpose flour to make a moderately stiff dough that is smooth and elastic (6 to 8 minutes total). Shape into a ball. Place in a lightly greased bowl; turn once to grease surface. Cover; let rise in a warm place till double (55 to 60 minutes). |
| | ● Punch down. Cover; let rest 10 minutes. Shape into a loaf. Place in a greased 8x4x2-inch loaf pan. Cover; let rise till nearly double (35 to 40 minutes). |
| | ● Bake in a 375° oven for 30 to 35 minutes. If necessary, cover top of loaf with foil during last 15 minutes of baking to prevent overbrowning. Remove from pan; cool on wire rack. Makes 1 loaf. |

**Start the day with a slice of toasted Swiss Rye Bread—for a change from cold cereal. Choose Swiss or cheddar cheese to team up with the distinctive flavor provided by rye or triticale flour.**

# Granary Bread

| | |
|---|---|
| **4 cups boiling water**<br>**½ cup cracked wheat**<br>**½ cup millet**<br>**⅓ cup molasses *or* honey**<br>**3 tablespoons cooking oil** | ● In saucepan combine boiling water, cracked wheat, and millet; simmer, covered, 5 minutes. Stir in molasses or honey and cooking oil. Let cool to lukewarm (110° to 115°). |
| **3 packages active dry yeast**<br>**½ cup rolled oats**<br>**½ cup cornmeal**<br>**½ cup nonfat dry milk powder**<br>**¼ cup toasted wheat germ *or* unprocessed wheat bran**<br>**2 teaspoons salt**<br>**1 cup walnuts *and/or* sunflower nuts** | ● Stir in yeast till dissolved. Add the ½ cup rolled oats, the cornmeal, the nonfat dry milk powder, the ¼ cup toasted wheat germ or unprocessed wheat bran, and the salt. Stir in the walnuts and/or the sunflower nuts. |
| **7 to 7½ cups whole wheat flour** | ● Using a spoon, stir in as much of the whole wheat flour as you can. Turn out onto lightly floured surface and knead in enough of the remaining flour to make a moderately stiff dough that is smooth and elastic (6 to 8 minutes total). Shape into a ball. Place dough in a lightly greased bowl; turn once to grease surface. Cover and let rise in warm place till double (about 1 hour). |
| **1 egg white**<br>**1 tablespoon water**<br>**Crushed rolled oats, toasted wheat germ, *or* unprocessed wheat bran** | ● Punch down; turn out onto floured surface. Divide in half. Cover; let rest 10 minutes. Shape into 2 loaves. Place in greased 9x5x3-inch loaf pans. Cover and let rise in warm place until nearly double (45 to 60 minutes). Make 3 diagonal slashes across top of each loaf. Brush tops with mixture of egg white and water; sprinkle with crushed oats, wheat germ, or bran. |
| | ● Bake in a 375° oven for 40 to 45 minutes. If necessary, cover tops of loaves with foil during the last 15 minutes to prevent overbrowning. Remove from pans and cool on wire rack. Makes 2 large loaves. |

If you want to try lots of whole grains in one loaf of bread, bake Granary Bread. Or if you have small amounts of whole grains to use up, this bread makes good use of them. Just remember that the bread will be coarser and much heavier than standard whole wheat loaves.

# Buckwheat Bread

| 3½ to 4 cups whole wheat flour<br>2 packages active dry yeast<br>1½ teaspoons salt | ● In a large mixer bowl stir together *2 cups* of the whole wheat flour, the yeast, and the salt. | **Brushing the loaf with the beaten egg white after baking gives it a crisp, shiny crust. But, if you'd rather have a soft crust, brush the loaf, before or after baking, with melted shortening, butter, margarine, or cooking oil.** |
|---|---|---|
| 1½ cups warm water (115° to 120°)<br>¼ cup honey<br>3 tablespoons cooking oil | ● Combine warm water, honey, and cooking oil. Add to flour mixture. Beat at low speed of electric mixer ½ minute, scraping sides of bowl constantly. Beat 3 minutes at high speed. | |
| 1¼ cups buckwheat flour | ● Using a spoon, stir in buckwheat flour and as much remaining whole wheat flour as you can. Turn out onto lightly floured surface. Knead in enough of the remaining whole wheat flour to make a moderately stiff dough that is smooth and elastic (6 to 8 minutes). Shape into a ball. Place in lightly greased bowl; turn once to grease surface. Cover; let rise in warm place till double (about 1 hour). | |
| | ● Punch dough down; turn out onto floured surface. Divide in half. Cover; let rest 10 minutes. Shape into two 5-inch round loaves and place on a greased baking sheet. Or, shape into 2 loaves and place in greased 8x4x2-inch loaf pans. Cover; let rise till nearly double (about 25 minutes). | |
| 1 slightly beaten egg white | ● Bake in a 375° oven for 25 to 30 minutes; cover top of loaf with foil after 15 minutes of baking to prevent overbrowning. Brush with egg white. Remove from pan; cool on wire rack. Makes 2 loaves. | |

# Pull-Apart Bread Loaves

| | |
|---|---|
| 2½ **cups boiling water**<br>½ **cup cracked wheat**<br>⅓ **cup steel-cut oats *or*<br>ground roasted<br>buckwheat groats<br>(kasha)** | ● In saucepan combine boiling water, cracked wheat, and steel-cut oats or buckwheat groats. Simmer, covered, about 10 minutes or till water is nearly absorbed. Cool till lukewarm. |
| 5 **to 5½ cups all-purpose<br>flour**<br>2 **packages active dry yeast** | ● In large mixer bowl combine *2 cups* of the all-purpose flour with the yeast. |
| 1 **cup milk**<br>6 **tablespoons butter *or*<br>margarine**<br>¼ **cup packed brown sugar**<br>2 **teaspoons salt** | ● In saucepan, heat the milk with butter or margarine, brown sugar, and salt just till warm (115° to 120°) and butter is almost melted; stir constantly. |
| 2 **eggs** | ● Add to flour mixture; add eggs and beat at low speed of electric mixer for ½ minute, scraping sides of bowl. Beat 3 minutes on high speed. |
| 2 **cups whole wheat flour** | ● Stir in cracked wheat mixture and whole wheat flour. Using a spoon, stir in as much of the remaining all-purpose flour as you can. Turn out onto lightly floured surface. Knead in enough of the remaining all-purpose flour to make a moderately stiff dough that is smooth and elastic (6 to 8 minutes). Shape into a ball. Place in a lightly greased bowl; turn once. Cover and let rise in warm place till double (50 to 60 minutes). |
| | ● Punch down. Cover; let rest 10 minutes. Divide into 30 pieces; shape into balls. Place six balls in *each* of five greased 7½x3½x2-inch loaf pans (see hint, above). Cover; let rise till nearly double (30 to 40 minutes). Bake according to directions opposite. |

This recipe makes plenty of bread for a crowd. But you may not have plenty of the 7½x3½x2-inch loaf pans for the baking. Instead, you can use three 9x5x3-inch loaf pans or three 9x1-inch round baking pans. Put 10 balls of dough in each pan and bake as directed for the smaller pans. Or use one 13x9x2-inch baking pan and one 9x5x3-inch loaf pan or 9x1-inch round baking pan. Put 20 balls of dough in the large pan and the remaining 10 in the smaller pan. Bake as directed in the recipe.

● Brush top of each loaf with water. Sprinkle top of each bun with a different topper. Bake in a 375° oven for 30 to 35 minutes, covering loaves with foil the last 10 minutes, if necessary, to prevent overbrowning. Remove from pans and cool on wire rack. Makes 5 loaves.

**Water**
**Assorted toppers (sesame seed, caraway seed, poppy seed, toasted wheat germ, rolled *or* steel-cut oats, cornmeal, coarse salt, dillweed, sunflower nuts, *or* finely chopped nuts)**

# Grain Sprouts Braided Loaf

| | | |
|---|---|---|
| **2 to 2½ cups whole wheat flour**<br>**1 package active dry yeast** | ● In a small mixer bowl combine *1 cup* of the whole wheat flour and the yeast. | 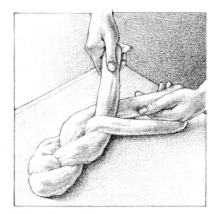 |
| **1 cup water**<br>**2 tablespoons sugar**<br>**2 tablespoons butter *or* margarine**<br>**1 teaspoon salt** | ● In saucepan heat water, sugar, butter, and salt just till warm (115° to 120°) and butter is almost melted; stir constantly. Add to flour mixture. Beat at low speed of electric mixer ½ minute, scraping bowl. Beat 3 minutes at high speed. | |
| **1 cup chopped wheat berry, rye berry, *or* brown rice sprouts (see tip, opposite)**<br>**2 tablespoons toasted wheat germ** | ● Using a spoon, stir in sprouts, wheat germ, and as much remaining whole wheat flour as you can. Turn out onto a lightly floured surface. Knead in enough of the remaining whole wheat flour to make a moderately stiff dough that is smooth and elastic (6 to 8 minutes total). Place in lightly greased bowl; turn once. Cover; let rise in a warm place till double (45 to 60 minutes). | **This bread tastes as good as it looks. Try this shaping method on other yeast loaves when you want to make an everyday bread look special. Divide dough into thirds and braid strands together, beginning in the middle and working toward each end. Pinch the ends together and tuck the sealed portion under the braid; place in loaf pan. Let rise into a braided beauty and bake as directed in your recipe.** |
| | ● Punch down; divide dough into 3 portions. Cover; let rest 10 minutes. Roll each piece into a 10-inch rope. Braid ropes together and secure ends. Place in a greased 8x4x2-inch loaf pan. Cover; let rise till nearly double (about 35 minutes). | |
| **Butter *or* margarine, melted** | ● Bake in a 375° oven 25 to 30 minutes. Cover loaf with foil the last 15 minutes, if necessary, to prevent overbrowning. Remove from pan to wire rack. Brush top lightly with melted butter or margarine. Cool. Makes 1 loaf. | |

# Homegrown Grain Sprouts

● Thoroughly wash ⅓ cup *wheat berries, rye berries,* or *brown rice*. Place grain kernels in a bowl and cover with enough water (about 1 inch) for grain to swell; cover. Let stand overnight in a cool place. Drain and rinse grain kernels.

Wash three 1-quart jars; place about ¼ cup of the soaked grain kernels in each jar. Cover tops of jars with two layers of cheesecloth or nylon netting. Fasten the cheesecloth on each jar with two rubber bands or a screw-top canning-jar lid band.

Place the jars on their sides in a warm, dark place (68° to 75° F). Once a day rinse the sprouts by pouring lukewarm water into the jars. Swirl to moisten all the grain kernels, then pour off the water. In three or four days, the grains should sprout. (Brown rice may take five to six days to sprout.)

Once grains have sprouted, keep refrigerated till serving time. Serve in salads, sandwiches, soups, or breads.

# Whole Wheat English Muffins

| | |
|---|---|
| 3 to 3½ cups all-purpose flour<br>1½ cups whole wheat flour<br>½ cup cracked wheat<br>2 packages active dry yeast | ● In large mixer bowl combine ¾ *cup* of the all-purpose flour, the whole wheat flour, the cracked wheat, and the yeast. |
| 2 cups milk<br>¼ cup shortening<br>2 tablespoons sugar<br>1½ teaspoons salt | ● In saucepan heat milk, shortening, sugar, and salt just till warm (115° to 120°), and shortening is almost melted; stir constantly. Add to dry mixture in mixer bowl. Beat at low speed of electric mixer for ½ minute, scraping bowl constantly. Beat 3 minutes at high speed. |
| | ● Using a spoon, stir in as much remaining all-purpose flour as you can. Turn out onto lightly floured surface; knead in enough remaining all-purpose flour to make a moderately stiff dough that is smooth and elastic (6 to 8 minutes). Place in greased bowl; turn once to grease surface. Cover; let rise in warm place till double (1 to 1¼ hours). Punch down. Cover; let rest 10 minutes. |
| Cornmeal | ● On lightly floured surface roll dough to slightly less than ½ inch thick. Cut with 4-inch round cutter, rerolling scraps. Dip both sides of muffins in cornmeal. (If necessary, lightly moisten muffins with water to make cornmeal adhere.) Cover; let rise about 30 minutes. |
| | ● Bake in ungreased electric skillet at 325° for 25 to 30 minutes or till muffins are done, turning frequently. Or, bake over low heat on ungreased griddle or skillet for 25 to 30 minutes, turning frequently. Cool thoroughly on wire rack. Makes 12 muffins. |

**On a lightly floured surface roll out the dough to slightly less than ½ inch thick. Cut with a 4-inch round cutter. Reroll any scraps.**

**Bake muffins in an ungreased electric skillet at 325° for 25 to 30 minutes or till muffins are done, turning frequently.**

# Chocolate-Rye Coffee Cake

| | |
|---|---|
| 4¼ to 4¾ cups all-purpose flour<br>1 cup rye *or* triticale flour<br>2 packages active dry yeast | ● In a large mixer bowl combine *1 cup* of the all-purpose flour, the rye flour, and the active dry yeast. |
| 1¼ cups milk<br>½ cup butter *or* margarine<br>½ cup packed brown sugar<br>½ cup semisweet chocolate pieces<br>½ teaspoon salt<br>2 eggs | ● In a saucepan heat milk, ½ cup butter, brown sugar, ½ cup chocolate pieces, and salt just till warm (115° to 120°) and butter is almost melted; stir constantly. Add to flour mixture; add eggs. Beat at low speed of electric mixer for ½ minute, scraping sides of bowl constantly. Beat 3 minutes at high speed. |
| | ● Using a spoon, stir in as much of the remaining all-purpose flour as you can. Turn out onto a lightly floured surface. Knead in enough of the remaining all-purpose flour to make a moderately soft dough that is smooth and elastic (3 to 5 minutes total). Shape into a ball. Place in lightly greased bowl; turn once to grease surface. Cover; let rise in warm place till double (about 2 hours). Punch dough down. Cover and let rest for 10 minutes. |
| 1 tablespoon butter *or* margarine, melted<br>½ cup semisweet chocolate pieces<br>¼ cup sugar<br>½ teaspoon ground cinnamon | ● Roll dough into an 18x12-inch rectangle. Spread 1 tablespoon melted butter over dough. Combine ½ cup chocolate pieces, sugar, and cinnamon. Sprinkle over dough. Roll up jelly-roll style, beginning from longest side. Join and seal ends. Place in a greased 10-inch tube pan. Cover; let rise till nearly double (about 1¼ hours). |
| | ● Bake on lower rack in a 350° oven for 45 to 50 minutes. Cool 15 minutes; remove from pan. Cool on wire rack. |
| 1 cup sifted powdered sugar<br>½ teaspoon butter *or* margarine<br>4 to 5 teaspoons hot water | ● Combine the powdered sugar, the ½ teaspoon butter or margarine, and enough water to make of glazing consistency. Spread on cooled coffee cake. Makes 1 large coffee cake. |

**Serve this coffee cake to mocha lovers. They may never guess that their favorite flavor is a subtle result of combining semisweet chocolate and rye flour. And there's a surprise inside, too. This special yeast coffee ring features a cinnamon sugar-chocolate filling.**

# Double-Oat Morning Buns

| | |
|---|---|
| ½ cup maple-flavored syrup<br>⅓ cup packed brown sugar<br>¼ cup butter *or* margarine | ● In saucepan combine syrup, the ⅓ cup brown sugar, and the ¼ cup butter or margarine. Cook and stir over low heat till brown sugar is dissolved; do not boil. Spread mixture in the bottom of a 13x9x2-inch baking pan. |
| 3 to 3½ cups all-purpose flour<br>1 package active dry yeast | ● In mixer bowl combine *2 cups* of the all-purpose flour and the yeast. |
| 1 cup milk<br>¼ cup sugar<br>¼ cup butter, margarine, *or* shortening<br>1 teaspoon salt<br>2 eggs | ● In saucepan heat milk, sugar, ¼ cup butter, and salt just till warm (115° to 120°); stir constantly. Add to flour mixture; add eggs. Beat at low speed of electric mixer for ½ minute, scraping sides of bowl constantly. Beat 3 minutes at high speed. |
| 1 cup oat flour (see tip, page 19) | ● Using a spoon, stir in the oat flour and as much of the remaining all-purpose flour as you can. Turn out onto lightly floured surface. Knead in enough of the remaining all-purpose flour to make a moderately stiff dough that is smooth and elastic (6 to 8 minutes total). Shape into a ball. Place in a lightly greased bowl; turn once to grease surface. Cover; let rise in warm place till double (1 to 1¼ hours). Punch down; divide in half. Cover; let rest 10 minutes. |
| 2 tablespoons melted butter *or* margarine<br>⅓ cup chopped nuts<br>¼ cup packed brown sugar<br>¼ cup toasted rolled oats (see tip, page 73)<br>¼ teaspoon ground cardamom<br>Butter *or* margarine, melted | ● Roll one half of dough into a 9x6-inch rectangle. Brush *1 tablespoon* of the melted butter over dough.<br>  Stir together the chopped nuts, the ¼ cup brown sugar, the toasted oats, and the ground cardamom; sprinkle half over the dough. Roll up jelly-roll style, beginning from the longest side. Pinch edges of dough together to seal firmly. Cut into 1-inch slices. Place, cut side down, in prepared pan. Repeat with remaining dough and filling.<br>  Brush rolls with additional melted butter. Cover with oiled waxed paper, then with clear plastic wrap. Refrigerate 2 to 24 hours. Remove rolls from refrigerator, uncover, and let stand about 20 minutes. Puncture any surface bubbles with a greased wooden pick. |
| | ● Bake in a 375° oven 20 to 25 minutes. Cool slightly; invert onto serving plate. Serve warm. Makes 18 buns. |

Double-Oat Morning Buns are worth getting up for. The oat flour produces a tender sweet roll that just melts in your mouth. And the ground cardamom adds an exotic touch. The rolled oats need to be toasted before you add them to the filling. That way they'll be soft and chewy after baking.
To make these buns without refrigerating, follow recipe as directed, *except do not* brush buns with the additional melted butter after they have been shaped and placed in the baking pan. Just cover the buns and let them rise at room temperature till nearly double (about 30 minutes). Bake them as directed in the recipe.

# Oatmeal-Raisin Rolls

2½ cups all-purpose flour
2 packages active dry yeast

● In a large mixer bowl combine the all-purpose flour and the yeast.

2 cups water
½ cup honey
¼ cup butter *or* margarine
½ teaspoon salt

● In a saucepan heat water, honey, butter or margarine, and salt till warm (115° to 120°); stir constantly. Add to flour mixture. Beat at low speed of electric mixer for ½ minute, scraping sides of bowl constantly. Beat 3 minutes at high speed.

1 cup rolled oats
1 cup unprocessed wheat bran
¾ cup raisins
2¾ to 3¼ cups whole wheat flour

● Stir in the rolled oats, the unprocessed wheat bran, and the raisins. Using a spoon, stir in as much of the whole wheat flour as you can. Turn out onto lightly floured surface. Knead in enough of the remaining whole wheat flour to make a moderately stiff dough that is smooth and elastic (6 to 8 minutes total). Shape into a ball. Place in a lightly greased bowl, turning once to grease surface. Cover; let rise in a warm place till double (45 to 60 minutes).

● Punch down; divide dough in half. Cover; let rest 10 minutes.
    Shape each half into 16 rolls; place on lightly greased baking sheet. Or, place 16 rolls in each of two greased 9x9x2-inch baking pans. Cover; let rise till nearly double (30 minutes).

● Bake in a 350° oven about 25 minutes. Cool on wire rack. Makes 32.

Here's how to serve yeast rolls piping hot the second time around. For reheating in the oven, place rolls in a brown paper bag; sprinkle the outside of the bag with water and fold the opening closed. Heat in a 325° oven for about 10 minutes or till rolls are heated through. Or, reheat rolls in aluminum foil, sprinkling rolls with water before wrapping.

# Whole Grain Dinner Rolls

2¾ to 3¼ cups all-purpose *or*
  whole wheat flour
1 package active dry yeast

½ cup milk
½ cup dairy sour cream
¼ cup honey
¼ cup butter *or* margarine
½ teaspoon salt
2 eggs
1 cup whole wheat, rye, oat,
  triticale, *or* buckwheat
  flour (see tip, page 19)
½ cup toasted wheat germ
  Butter *or* margarine,
  melted (optional)

● In large mixer bowl combine *1½ cups* of the all-purpose flour and the yeast.

● Heat milk, sour cream, honey, butter, and salt till warm (115° to 120°) and butter is almost melted. Add to flour mixture; add eggs. Beat at low speed of electric mixer ½ minute, scraping bowl. Beat 3 minutes at high speed.

  Using a spoon stir in the 1 cup whole wheat flour, wheat germ, and as much of the remaining all-purpose flour as you can. Turn out onto lightly floured surface. Knead in enough of the remaining all-purpose flour to make a moderately stiff dough that is smooth and elastic (6 to 8 minutes total). Shape into a ball. Place in lightly greased bowl; turn once. Cover; let rise in a warm place till double (about 1 hour).

  Punch down; divide dough in half. Cover; let rest 10 minutes. Shape into Rosettes (see directions, right), Parker House Rolls, Cloverleaf Rolls, or Hamburger Buns (see shaping directions, page 46). Cover; let rise till nearly double (about 30 minutes). Bake in a 375° oven for 13 to 15 minutes. Brush with melted butter, if desired. Makes 24 to 30 rolls.

**For *Rosettes* (see photo, below): divide each half of dough into 12 pieces. On lightly floured surface, roll each piece into a 12-inch rope. Tie in a loose knot, leaving two long ends. Tuck one end under each roll. Bring other end up; tuck in top center of roll. Place 2 to 3 inches apart on greased baking sheets. Let rise; bake as directed. Makes 24.**

● **Whole Grain Brown-and-Serve
Rolls:** Prepare Whole Grain
Dinner Rolls as directed, opposite, *except*
bake in a 325° oven about 10 minutes;
*do not brown.* Remove from pans; cool
on wire rack. Wrap in moisture-
vaporproof material making packages of
desired number of rolls to suit your
serving needs. Seal, label, and freeze.

　　To serve, open wrapping. Thaw rolls
in wrapping at room temperature for 10
to 15 minutes. Unwrap completely. Bake
on ungreased baking sheets in a 375°
oven for 10 to 15 minutes. Serve warm.

# Dinner Roll Shaping

*See recipe and photo, pages 44 and 45—*

● **Parker House Rolls:** Lightly grease baking sheets. On lightly floured surface, roll out each half of dough to ¼-inch thickness. Cut with floured 2½-inch round cutter. Brush with melted *butter*. Make an off-center crease in each round. Fold so large half slightly overlaps small half (see photo, right). Place rolls 2 to 3 inches apart on baking sheets. Let rise and bake as directed on page 44. Makes 30 rolls.

● **Cloverleaves:** Lightly grease 24 muffin cups. Divide each half of dough into 36 pieces. Shape each piece into a ball, pulling edges under to make a smooth top. Place 3 balls in each greased muffin cup, smooth side up (see photo, right). Let rise and bake as directed on page 44. Makes 24.

● **Hamburger Buns:** Lightly grease baking sheet. Prepare dough as directed on page 44, *except* do not divide in half after punching down. Instead, divide dough into 12 portions. Cover; let rest 10 minutes. Shape each portion into an even circle, folding edges under. Press flat between hands. Place on baking sheet; press into 3½-inch circles. Cover; let rise till nearly double (about 30 minutes). If desired, brush buns with mixture of 1 beaten *egg white* and 1 tablespoon *water;* sprinkle tops lightly with toasted wheat germ or sesame seed. With a sharp knife, make 5 slashes on tops of buns from center to outside edges, forming a star-shape design. Bake as directed on page 44. Makes 12 buns.

● **Crescent Rolls:** Lightly grease baking sheets. On lightly floured surface, roll each half of dough into a 12-inch circle. Brush with melted *butter*. Cut each circle into 12 wedges. To shape, begin at wide end of wedge and roll toward point (see photo, right). Place, point side down, 2 to 3 inches apart on baking sheets. Let rise and bake as directed on page 44. Makes 24 rolls.

# Bran-Bulgur Crescents

|  |  |
|---|---|
| ½ cup bulgur wheat<br>1 cup boiling water | ● In saucepan combine bulgur and boiling water. Simmer, covered, for 5 minutes. Drain well; set aside. |
| 3½ to 4 cups all-purpose flour<br>2 packages active dry yeast | ● In large mixing bowl combine *1½ cups* of the flour and the yeast. |
| 1 cup milk<br>⅓ cup honey<br>¼ cup butter *or* margarine<br>2 teaspoons salt<br>½ cup unprocessed wheat bran | ● In saucepan heat milk, honey, ¼ cup butter, and salt just till warm (115° to 120°) and butter is almost melted; stir constantly. Add to flour mixture. Beat at low speed of electric mixer for ½ minute, scraping sides of bowl constantly. Beat 3 minutes at high speed. Stir in the bran and cooked bulgur. |
| | ● Using a spoon, stir in as much of the remaining flour as you can. Turn out onto a lightly floured surface. Knead in enough of the remaining flour to make a moderately stiff dough that is smooth and elastic (6 to 8 minutes total). Shape into a ball. Place in a lightly greased bowl; turn once to grease surface. Cover and let rise in warm place till double (about 1½ hours).<br>  Punch down; turn out onto lightly floured surface. Divide dough into 3 equal portions; shape each into a ball. Cover and let rest 10 minutes. |
| 3 tablespoons butter *or* margarine, softened | ● Lightly grease baking sheets. On a lightly floured surface roll one ball of dough into a 12-inch circle. Spread with *1 tablespoon* of the softened butter; cut circle into 12 wedges. To shape rolls, begin at wide end of wedge and roll toward point. Place, point down, 2 to 3 inches apart on baking sheet. Repeat with remaining 2 balls of dough. Cover rolls; let rise in warm place till nearly double (20 to 30 minutes). |
| 3 tablespoons butter *or* margarine, melted | ● Brush rolls with the 3 tablespoons melted butter. Bake in a 400° oven for 10 to 12 minutes or till done. Remove from baking sheet; cool on a wire rack. Brush again with additional melted butter, if desired. Makes 36 rolls. |

**Take a favorite—like crescent rolls—and surprise everyone with the good taste and texture that unprocessed bran and bulgur wheat can add. These buttery treats are a perfect way to introduce whole grains.**

# Wheat Berry-Minestrone Soup

| | |
|---|---|
| 3½  cups water<br>½  cup wheat berries | ● In a saucepan combine water and wheat berries. Bring to boiling; reduce heat. Simmer, covered, for 1 hour. |
| 1  15-ounce can great northern beans<br>1  10½-ounce can condensed beef broth<br>1  7½-ounce can tomatoes, cut up<br>1  cup loose-pack frozen carrot, cauliflower, green beans, zucchini, and butter beans<br>½  cup chopped onion<br>2  tablespoons snipped parsley<br>1  teaspoon dried basil, crushed<br>1  clove garlic, minced | ● Add the great northern beans, the beef broth, the *undrained* tomatoes, the frozen vegetables, the chopped onion, the snipped parsley, the basil, and the garlic. Bring to boiling; reduce heat. Simmer, covered, for 15 to 20 minutes or till vegetables are tender. |
| Grated Parmesan cheese | ● Serve in soup bowls. Sprinkle each serving with Parmesan cheese. Makes 6 to 8 servings. |

**Minestrone with a difference—that's what you taste with this soup. Wheat berries add a pleasant, chewy surprise in the bottom of your soup bowl.**

# Freezing Grain Berries

Keep a supply of cooked wheat, rye, or triticale berries in your freezer so you can add them to your favorite recipes at a moment's notice. Prepare grain berries as directed on pages 8 and 9, being certain to drain berries well after cooking. Place recipe-size portions (for example, ¼-cup, ½-cup, or 1-cup sizes) in freezer containers. Label and freeze for up to 3 months. To quickly thaw frozen berries, put in a colander and rinse under hot tap water for a few minutes.

# Creamy Corn Soup with Cornmeal Toppers

1 cup water
½ cup yellow cornmeal
2 tablespoons grated Parmesan cheese
1 teaspoon butter *or* margarine
1 tablespoon snipped parsley

● For cornmeal toppers, combine water, cornmeal, Parmesan cheese, and 1 teaspoon butter. Cook and stir till thickened. Remove from heat.
　Stir in parsley. Drop in 6 equal mounds onto a greased baking sheet. Bake in a 400° oven for 25 minutes. Remove to wire rack.

½ cup chopped celery
¼ cup chopped onion
1 tablespoon butter *or* margarine

● Meanwhile, in a saucepan cook celery and onion in 1 tablespoon butter till onion is tender but not brown.

**Just before serving, gently place a cornmeal topper atop each bowl of hot, creamy soup.**

3 cups chicken broth
1 10-ounce package frozen whole kernel corn *or* 2 cups fresh whole kernel corn
½ cup sliced carrots

● Add broth, corn, and carrots. Bring to boiling; reduce heat. Simmer, covered, for 10 to 12 minutes.

1 cup light cream

● Stir in the light cream; heat through. Pour soup into serving bowls.
　Place one warm cornmeal topper atop soup in each bowl. Makes 6 servings.

# Mushroom-Rice Soup

| | |
|---|---|
| **4 cups beef broth**<br>**¼ cup chopped onion**<br>**¼ cup chopped green pepper**<br>**1 tablespoon snipped parsley** | ● In a saucepan combine beef broth, onion, green pepper, and parsley. Bring to boiling; reduce heat. Simmer, uncovered, for 15 minutes. |
| **¼ cup wild rice** | ● Run cold water over *uncooked* rice in a strainer for 1 minute, lifting rice with fingers to rinse well. Add to beef broth. Simmer, covered, for 40 minutes. |
| **1 cup sliced fresh mushrooms**<br>**⅓ cup dry white *or* red wine** | ● Add mushrooms and wine. Simmer, covered, for 20 minutes more or till rice is tender. Makes 4 to 6 servings. |

For a first-course sure to please, serve Mushroom-Rice Soup. It features wild rice—a North American aquatic grass unrelated to rice—in a delicate wine-flavored broth.

# Cracked Wheat and Broccoli Chowder

| | | |
|---|---|---|
| **1 10-ounce package frozen cut broccoli** | ● Cook broccoli according to package directions. Drain. | **Cracked wheat, cracked rye, or steel-cut oats add the texture to this creamy yet crunchy soup. And because you only need a little bit, it's a great way to use up small amounts of grains.** |
| **2 cups chicken broth**<br>**⅓ cup cracked wheat, cracked rye, *or* steel-cut oats**<br>**¼ cup chopped onion**<br>**½ teaspoon salt**<br>**⅛ teaspoon ground nutmeg** | ● In a saucepan combine *1½ cups* of the chicken broth; cracked wheat, cracked rye, or steel-cut oats; chopped onion; salt; and ground nutmeg. Bring mixture to boiling; reduce heat. Simmer, covered, for 10 minutes or till the grain is tender. | |
| | ● Meanwhile, in a food processor bowl or blender container combine *half* of the broccoli and the remaining chicken broth. Cover and process or blend 30 to 60 seconds or till smooth. | |
| **2 cups milk**<br>**3 tablespoons all-purpose *or* whole wheat flour**<br>**1 tablespoon butter *or* margarine** | ● Combine the milk and flour; add to grain mixture. Cook and stir till mixture is thickened and bubbly. Stir in the broccoli pieces, pureed broccoli, and the butter or margarine. Cook and stir till soup is heated through. Season to taste with salt and pepper. Serves 4 to 6. | |

# Whole Grain Flours as Thickeners

Oat, brown rice, whole wheat, rye, buckwheat, or triticale flours are ideal thickeners for sauces or gravies. Substitute equal amounts of whole grain flour for all-purpose flour in your recipes. The sauce consistencies will be the same as those made with all-purpose flour. You will notice a difference in color and flavor. Sauces made with whole grain flours will be somewhat darker and have a more distinctive flavor than traditional sauces.

# Whole Wheat Pastry

| | |
|---|---|
| ¾ **cup whole wheat flour**<br>½ **cup all-purpose flour**<br>½ **teaspoon salt** | ● In a mixing bowl stir together whole wheat flour, all-purpose flour, and salt. |

**To transfer rolled pie-crust easily to the pie plate, wrap crust around a rolling pin. Slowly unroll it onto the pie plate.**

| | |
|---|---|
| ⅓ **cup shortening** *or* **lard**<br>3 **to 4 tablespoons cold milk** | ● Cut in shortening or lard till pieces are the size of small peas. Sprinkle *1 tablespoon* of the milk over part of the mixture; gently toss with a fork. Push to side of bowl. Repeat till all is moistened. Form dough into a ball. On a lightly floured surface, flatten dough with hands. Roll dough from center to edge, forming a circle about 12 inches in diameter. |

● Wrap the pastry around a rolling pin. Unroll onto a 9-inch pie plate. Being careful not to stretch dough, ease pastry into pie plate. Trim to ½ inch beyond edge of pie plate; fold under extra pastry. Flute the edge. Do not prick pastry. Bake as directed in individual recipe. Makes 1 pie shell.

**Baked Pastry Shell:** Prepare pastry as above, *except* prick bottom and sides with the tines of a fork. Bake in a 450° oven for 10 to 12 minutes or till golden. Cool on a wire rack.

**Team up your favorite pie or quiche fillings with the Whole Wheat Pastry crust variation that suits your fancy and your recipe.**

**Double-Crust Pastry:** Prepare pastry as above, *except* use 1½ cups *whole wheat flour,* 1 cup *all-purpose flour,* 1 teaspoon *salt,* ⅔ cup *shortening* or *lard,* and 6 to 7 tablespoons *cold milk.* Divide dough in half. Roll out half of dough as above. Fit into pie plate. Trim pastry even with rim. For top crust, roll out remaining dough. Cut slits for escape of steam. Place *desired pie filling* in pie shell. Top with pastry for top crust. Trim top crust ½ inch beyond edge of pie plate. Fold extra pastry under bottom crust; flute edge. Bake as directed in individual recipe.

**Savory Whole Wheat Pastry:** Prepare pastry as directed, *except* combine ¼ teaspoon desired *dried herb,* crushed, with the flour-salt mixture for single-crust pastry or ½ teaspoon desired *dried herb,* crushed, for the double-crust pastry. Use basil, thyme, rosemary, or dillweed.

# Wheat Berry Quiche

| | |
|---|---|
| **Whole Wheat Pastry (see recipe, opposite)** | ● Prepare pastry as directed. Line pastry shell with a double thickness of heavy-duty foil. Press down firmly but gently. Bake in a 450° oven for 5 minutes. Remove foil; set crust aside. Lower oven temperature to 375°. |
| ½ **cup sliced fresh mushrooms**<br>¼ **cup chopped green pepper**<br>¼ **cup shredded carrot**<br>1 **tablespoon butter *or* margarine** | ● In a skillet cook the sliced mushrooms, chopped green pepper, and shredded carrot in the butter or margarine till vegetables are tender but not brown. |
| 4 **beaten eggs**<br>1 **cup light cream**<br>½ **cup milk**<br>½ **teaspoon salt**<br>½ **teaspoon dried basil, crushed** | ● In a mixing bowl stir together the beaten eggs, the light cream, the milk, the salt, and the dried basil. |
| 1½ **cups shredded Monterey Jack cheese (6 ounces)**<br>1 **cup cooked wheat, rye, *or* triticale berries (see cooking directions, pages 8 and 9)** | ● Stir in the cooked vegetables and cheese. Sprinkle cooked wheat berries in bottom of pastry shell. Pour in egg mixture. Bake in a 375° oven about 30 minutes or till knife inserted near center comes out clean. Let stand on wire rack 5 minutes before serving. Serves 6. |

**Wheat berries add a layer of chewy goodness under the creamy egg-cheese-vegetable filling.**

# Crunchy New Orleans-Style Rice Patties

1½ **cups cooked brown rice (see cooking directions, page 9), slightly cooled**
2 **beaten eggs**
½ **cup sliced green onion**
½ **cup chopped walnuts**
¼ **cup fine dry bread crumbs**
1 **tablespoon chopped pimiento**
½ **teaspoon dried thyme, crushed**
¼ **teaspoon dried basil, crushed**
⅛ **teaspoon salt**
**Several dashes ground red pepper**

● In a medium bowl combine the cooked and slightly cooled brown rice, the beaten eggs, the sliced green onion, the chopped walnuts, the fine dry bread crumbs, the chopped pimiento, the dried thyme, the dried basil, the salt, and the ground red pepper.

Shape the rice mixture into eight ½-inch-thick patties. (Moisten hands to form patties, if necessary.)

2 **tablespoons cooking oil**

● In a large skillet over medium heat, fry the rice patties in hot cooking oil till golden brown, allowing 3 to 4 minutes per side. Remove to platter; keep warm.

¼ **cup chopped green pepper**
1 **tablespoon butter *or* margarine**
1 **15½-ounce can red kidney beans**
1 **8-ounce can tomato sauce**
1 **teaspoon chili powder**
1 **cup shredded cheddar cheese (4 ounces)**
¼ **cup dairy sour cream**

● Meanwhile, for sauce, in a saucepan cook green pepper in butter or margarine till tender. Stir in *undrained* beans, tomato sauce, and chili powder. Simmer, uncovered, about 6 minutes or till heated through. Mash beans slightly.

Spoon some of the bean mixture atop each patty. Sprinkle with some of the cheddar cheese and dollop with sour cream. Makes 4 servings.

**Brown rice patties with red bean sauce was inspired by Creole red beans and rice. The New Orleans original was usually served on Mondays, which were washdays. The beans and rice cooked all day as folks waited for their laundry to dry. You don't have to wait all day to enjoy our version.**

# Spinach-Millet Soufflé

| | |
|---|---|
| 2 cups water<br>⅓ cup millet | ● Attach a foil collar to a 2-quart soufflé dish (see hint, right). Set aside.<br>    In saucepan combine water and millet. Simmer, covered, for 10 minutes; drain. |
| 8 ounces fresh spinach *or* one 10-ounce package frozen chopped spinach | ● In a saucepan, cook fresh spinach, covered, in a small amount of boiling salted water for 3 to 5 minutes. (*Or,* cook frozen spinach according to package directions.) Drain well. |
| ¼ cup chopped onion<br>¼ cup butter *or* margarine<br>¼ cup all-purpose flour<br>¼ teaspoon ground nutmeg<br>1 cup milk<br>1½ cups shredded Swiss cheese (6 ounces) | ● In a saucepan cook onion in butter till the onion is tender but not brown. Stir in flour and nutmeg. Add milk all at once. Cook; stir till thickened and bubbly. Cook and stir 1 minute more. Remove from heat. Add cheese and cooked millet; stir to melt cheese. Stir in spinach. |
| 6 egg yolks<br>6 egg whites | ● Beat egg yolks till thick and lemon-colored. Slowly add cheese mixture to egg yolks; stir constantly. Cool slightly. Using *clean* beaters, beat egg whites till stiff peaks form. Gradually pour yolk mixture over beaten whites, folding to blend. Turn out into prepared ungreased 2-quart soufflé dish. |

● Bake in a 350° oven for 50 to 55 minutes or till a knife inserted near center comes out clean. *Do not* open oven door till near the end of the baking time. Test soufflé while soufflé is in oven. Gently peel off collar; serve immediately. Serves 6.

**To attach a foil collar to the soufflé dish, cut a piece of foil long enough to wrap around the dish with a 2- to 3-inch overlap. Fold foil into thirds lengthwise. Butter one side. Position foil around dish with buttered side in, letting collar extend 2 inches above top of dish; fasten with tape.**

# Pork and Barley Stew

| | |
|---|---|
| ½ **pound boneless pork, cut into 1-inch cubes**<br>1 **tablespoon cooking oil**<br>1 **cup tomato juice**<br>1 **7½-ounce can tomatoes, cut up**<br>1 **cup beer**<br>½ **cup chopped onion**<br>2 **tablespoons brown sugar**<br>2 **tablespoons vinegar**<br>½ **teaspoon dried thyme, crushed**<br>¼ **teaspoon salt**<br>¼ **teaspoon pepper** | ● In a large saucepan brown pork in the hot cooking oil; drain fat.<br>　Add the tomato juice, the *undrained* tomatoes, the beer, the chopped onion, the brown sugar, the vinegar, the dried thyme, the salt, and the pepper.<br>　Bring to boiling; reduce heat and simmer, covered, for 30 minutes. |
| ½ **pound smoked bratwurst, cut into 1-inch pieces**<br>⅓ **cup pearl barley**<br>1 **medium zucchini, cut into ¼-inch slices** | ● Add bratwurst and barley. Simmer, covered, for 30 minutes.<br>　Add zucchini. Simmer, covered, for 15 minutes more or till barley is done. Makes 4 servings. |

You'll be getting barley in more than one way with this chunky stew. Though most recognizable in soups, cereals, or salads, barley also is used to produce the malt for brewing beer.

# Barley-Stuffed Steaks

| | |
|---|---|
| 1 **cup water**<br>⅓ **cup pearl barley**<br>¼ **cup sliced green onion** | ● In saucepan combine water and barley. Bring to boiling; reduce heat. Simmer, covered, for 30 minutes. Drain well. Add green onion. |
| 4 **ounces braunschweiger**<br>1 **tablespoon milk**<br>1 **tablespoon Dijon-style mustard**<br>1 **clove garlic, minced**<br>¼ **teaspoon salt** | ● Combine the braunschweiger, the milk, the Dijon-style mustard, the minced garlic, and the salt; mix well. |
| 4 **beef top loin steaks, cut 1 to 1¼ inches thick** | ● Slash fat edge of each steak at 1-inch intervals (don't cut into meat). Slice a pocket in the other side of each steak; spread ¼ of the braunschweiger mixture in bottom side of each pocket. Stuff with ¼ of the barley mixture. |
| | ● Place steaks on unheated rack of broiler pan. Broil about 3 inches from heat to desired doneness, turning once. (Allow 12 to 14 minutes total time for medium.) Transfer steaks to a heated serving platter. Makes 8 servings. |

Cut a pocket in the side of the steak opposite the side with the fat edges. Use a sharp knife to slit steak almost through to opposite side and about ½ inch in from each end.

# Rice Pilaf Salad

⅓ cup wine vinegar
2 teaspoons dry mustard
1 teaspoon lemon juice
1 teaspoon sugar
1 teaspoon salt
½ teaspoon paprika
2 small cloves garlic, minced
  Dash ground red pepper

● For dressing, combine the wine vinegar, dry mustard, lemon juice, sugar, salt, paprika, minced garlic, and ground red pepper; mix well.

**If you like the way brown rice adds texture to this entrée, think about substituting it for white rice in other recipes. But expect some differences. Brown rice will always be chewier than white rice and will require a longer cooking time.**

2 cups chopped cooked beef
1¼ cups cooked brown rice (see cooking directions, page 9)
1 cup canned garbanzo beans
1 8-ounce can red kidney beans, drained
1 apple, chopped
½ cup sliced celery
1 small green pepper, chopped
¼ cup sliced pitted ripe olives
¼ cup sliced green onion
¼ cup snipped parsley

● In a large bowl stir together the chopped cooked beef, the cooked brown rice, the garbanzo beans, the kidney beans, the chopped apple, the sliced celery, the chopped green pepper, the sliced ripe olives, the sliced green onion, and the snipped parsley.
  Pour dressing over the beef-rice mixture. Cover; chill.

1 apple, cored and sliced
2 hard-cooked eggs, sliced
  Fresh alfalfa sprouts
½ cup sunflower nuts

● To serve beef-rice mixture, arrange on platter with apple slices, egg slices, and alfalfa sprouts. Sprinkle the sunflower nuts atop. Makes 6 servings.

# Any-Grain Pizza Crust

1½ to 2 cups all-purpose flour
¾ cup whole wheat, rye, *or* oat flour (see tip, page 19)
¼ cup toasted wheat germ *or* cornmeal
1 package active dry yeast
1 teaspoon salt
1 cup warm water (115° to 120°)
2 tablespoons cooking oil

● In mixer bowl combine ¾ *cup* of all-purpose flour, the whole wheat flour, wheat germ, yeast, and salt. Stir in water and oil. Beat at low speed of electric mixer for ½ minute, scraping bowl. Beat 3 minutes at high speed. Using a spoon, stir in as much of the remaining all-purpose flour as you can. Turn out onto lightly floured surface. Knead in enough remaining all-purpose flour to make a moderately stiff dough that is smooth and elastic (6 to 8 minutes total).

To make a 14-inch deep-dish pizza like the one shown at right, prepare thick-crust pizza as directed, *except* do not divide dough in half before shaping. Roll dough into 16-inch circle and pat in pan. Let rise and bake as directed.

Cornmeal

**For a thick crust:** Place dough in greased bowl; turn once. Cover; let rise till double (about 1 hour). Punch down. Cover; let rest 10 minutes. Sprinkle two greased 9x9x2-inch baking pans or 10-inch ovenproof skillets with cornmeal. With greased fingers pat dough into bottom and halfway up the sides. Cover; let rise till nearly double (30 to 45 minutes). Bake in a 375° oven for 20 to 25 minutes or till light brown. To assemble pizza, see directions, right.
**For a thin crust:** Divide dough in half. Cover; let rest 10 minutes. Sprinkle two 12-inch greased pizza pans with cornmeal. On lightly floured surface roll each dough half into a 13-inch circle; transfer to pans. Build up edges. Bake in a 425° oven for 12 minutes. To assemble pizza, see directions, right.

**To assemble:** Top pizza
crusts with desired pizza ingredients (see
recipes, pages 60 and 61).
For *thick-crust* pizza, bake in a 375° oven
20 to 25 minutes or till bubbly.
For *thin-crust* pizza, bake in a 425° oven
10 to 15 minutes. Makes 2 pizzas.

# Italian-Style Pizza

| | |
|---|---|
| Any-Grain Pizza Crust (see recipe, page 58) | ● Prepare thick or thin pizza crusts. |
| 1  15-ounce can tomato sauce<br>1  cup chopped green pepper<br>1  cup chopped onion<br>1  tablespoon snipped parsley<br>1  teaspoon dried basil, crushed<br>1  teaspoon dried oregano, crushed<br>1  clove garlic, minced | ● For sauce, in a saucepan combine the tomato sauce, the chopped green pepper, the chopped onion, the snipped parsley, the dried basil, the dried oregano, and the minced garlic.<br>  Bring to boiling; reduce heat. Simmer, uncovered, for 5 minutes. Spread the tomato sauce atop pizza crusts. |
| ½  cup grated Parmesan cheese (2 ounces) | ● Sprinkle the grated Parmesan cheese atop pizzas. |
| 1  pound bulk Italian sausage, cooked and drained<br>1  2-ounce jar sliced pimiento<br>2  4-ounce cans sliced mushrooms, drained (optional)<br>¼  cup chopped green olives (optional)<br>2  cups shredded mozzarella cheese (8 ounces) | ● Sprinkle cooked bulk Italian sausage and sliced pimiento atop Parmesan cheese. Sprinkle sliced mushrooms and chopped green olives over pizzas, if desired. Sprinkle the shredded mozzarella cheese atop pizzas. Bake according to directions on page 59. Makes 2 pizzas. |

Add your own personal style to Italian-Style Pizza. If you don't want to use Italian sausage, substitute 6 ounces of sliced pepperoni for a different look and taste. Or add sliced pitted ripe olives to replace all or part of the green olives.

# German-Style Pizza

| | |
|---|---|
| Any-Grain Pizza Crust (see recipe, page 58) | ● Prepare thick or thin pizza crusts. |
| 1  8-ounce can tomato sauce<br>1  7½-ounce can tomatoes, cut up<br>½  cup chopped onion<br>½  cup beer<br>¼  teaspoon dried thyme, crushed | ● For sauce, in a saucepan combine tomato sauce, tomatoes, chopped onion, beer, and dried thyme. Bring to boiling; reduce heat. Simmer, uncovered, for 20 minutes. Spread atop pizza crusts. |
| 3  cups shredded Swiss cheese (12 ounces) | ● Sprinkle one-third of the cheese over the pizzas. |
| 1  8-ounce can sauerkraut, drained and snipped<br>2  teaspoons caraway seed | ● Combine sauerkraut and caraway seed. Arrange atop cheese layer. |
| 1  8-ounce package fully cooked smoked sausage links, thinly sliced | ● Arrange sausage slices atop sauerkraut layer. Top with the remaining cheese. Bake according to directions on page 59. Makes 2 pizzas. |

Make pizza crusts ahead, so they'll be ready when you are. Cool crusts completely on wire racks after the first baking, then remove them from the pans. Wrap them in moisture- and vaporproof material, label, and freeze for up to 8 months. Thaw the wrapped crusts at room temperature about 30 minutes and complete making the pizzas as directed in the recipe.

# Mexican-Style Pizza

| Any-Grain Pizza Crust (see recipe, page 58) | ● Prepare thick or thin pizza crusts. |
| --- | --- |
| 3 cups shredded cheddar *or* Monterey Jack cheese | ● Sprinkle *half* of the shredded cheese atop pizza crusts. |
| 1 pound ground beef<br>½ cup chopped onion<br>1 10-ounce can tomatoes and green chili peppers<br>½ teaspoon chili powder<br>¼ teaspoon garlic salt | ● Cook ground beef and onion till beef is brown and onion is tender. Drain off fat. Stir in tomatoes and green chili peppers, chili powder, and garlic salt. Spread meat mixture atop cheese. Sprinkle remaining cheese atop meat. Bake pizzas according to the directions on page 59. |
| 1 cup shredded lettuce<br>2 medium tomatoes, chopped<br>½ cup sliced pitted ripe olives<br>Bottled taco sauce *or* hot pepper sauce | ● Before serving, sprinkle lettuce atop pizzas; arrange chopped tomatoes and sliced olives atop. Pass taco or pepper sauce. Makes 2 pizzas. |

This pizza is like an open-face tostada. Let folks layer their own pieces of hot-from-the-oven pizza with as much lettuce, chopped tomato, and olives as they want. And pass the taco or hot pepper sauce for those with iron-lined stomachs!

1) German-Style Pizza
2) Italian-Style Pizza
3) Mexican-Style Pizza

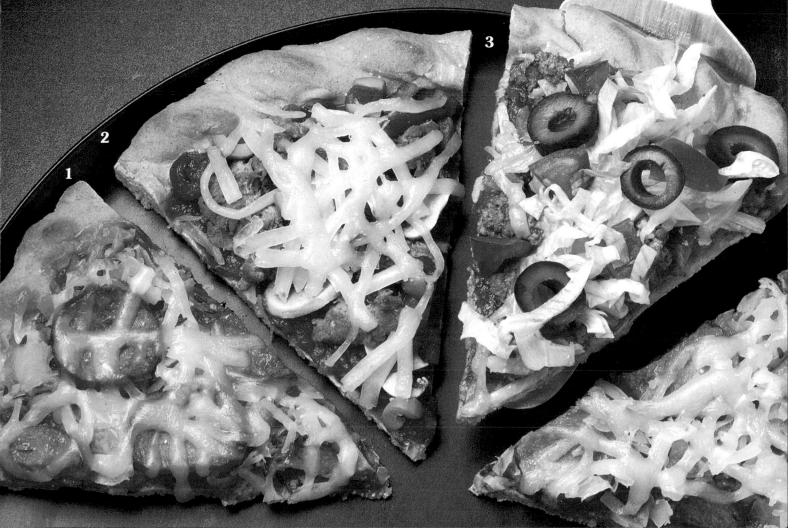

# Bulgur Burgers with Yogurt Sauce

| | |
|---|---|
| 1 beaten egg<br>⅓ cup bulgur wheat<br>1 tablespoon snipped parsley *or* 1 teaspoon dried parsley flakes<br>½ teaspoon dry mustard<br>¼ teaspoon salt<br>¼ teaspoon pepper<br>1 pound ground beef | ● In a bowl combine egg, bulgur wheat, parsley, mustard, salt, and pepper. Add beef; mix well.<br>　Shape into four ½-inch-thick patties. Place patties on an unheated rack in a broiler pan. Broil 3 inches from heat to desired doneness, turning once (allow about 8 minutes total time for rare; about 10 minutes for medium; about 12 minutes for well done). |
| 2 tablespoons plain yogurt<br>1 tablespoon mayonnaise *or* salad dressing<br>⅛ teaspoon ground coriander<br>1 small tomato, peeled, seeded, and chopped<br>¼ cup thinly sliced green onion | ● For sauce, in a bowl stir together the plain yogurt, the mayonnaise or salad dressing, and the ground coriander.<br>　Stir in the chopped tomato and thinly sliced green onion. |
| Lettuce leaves<br>4 Hamburger Buns, split, toasted, and buttered (see recipe, pages 44 and 46) | ● To serve, place a lettuce leaf on bun bottom; top with a beef patty. Spoon some of the sauce over patty. Top with bun top. Repeat to make 4 sandwiches. Makes 4 servings. |

**Bulgur Burgers are great barbecued, too. Grill burgers over *medium-hot* coals for 5 to 6 minutes; turn and grill 4 to 5 minutes more.**
**For a different look, substitute an onion slice and tomato slice for the green onion and chopped tomato. Layer with the burger and drizzle with the sauce mixture.**

# Cornmeal Crepes

| | |
|---|---|
| ¾ cup milk<br>⅓ cup yellow cornmeal<br>3 tablespoons all-purpose flour<br>1 egg<br>2 teaspoons cooking oil | ● In a mixing bowl stir together the milk, yellow cornmeal, all-purpose flour, egg, and cooking oil. Beat with a rotary beater till well mixed. |
| | ● Heat a lightly greased 6-inch skillet. Remove from heat. Spoon in about *2 tablespoons* batter; lift and tilt skillet to spread batter evenly. Return to heat; brown one side only. Invert pan over paper toweling; remove crepe. Repeat to make 8 crepes; grease pan occasionally. Stir batter frequently to keep cornmeal from settling. Makes 8 crepes. |

**Tired of the same old tortillas in Mexican-style casseroles? Substitute cornmeal crepes as we did. The recipe is easily doubled if you want to use these crepes instead of tortillas in your favorite recipes.**

# Mexicali Crepes

**Cornmeal Crepes (see recipe, opposite)**

● Prepare crepes as directed; set aside.

1 **10-ounce can tomatoes and jalapeños**
2 **teaspoons cornstarch**
2 **tablespoons chopped green pepper**
¼ **teaspoon pepper**
  **Few dashes bottled hot pepper sauce (optional)**

● For sauce, in a small saucepan combine *undrained* tomatoes and cornstarch. Stir in green pepper, pepper, and hot pepper sauce, if desired. Cook and stir till thickened and bubbly; cook and stir 2 minutes more.

**Look in the Mexican food section at the grocery store for canned tomatoes with jalapeños. They add a hint of hotness to this sauce. If you want a spicier sauce, sprinkle in the hot pepper sauce as liberally as you dare.**

¾ **pound ground beef**
¼ **cup chopped onion**
1 **small clove garlic, minced**
¼ **cup tomato paste**
½ **teaspoon chili powder**
¼ **teaspoon salt**
1½ **cups shredded cheddar cheese (6 ounces)**
  **Fresh hot peppers**
  **Cherry tomatoes**

● In skillet cook beef, onion, and garlic till meat is brown; drain off fat. Stir in tomato paste, chili powder, salt, and ¼ *cup* of the sauce. Spread about ¼ *cup* of the meat mixture in the center of each crepe; top with *1 tablespoon* of the cheese. Roll up and place seam side down in a 10x6x2-inch baking dish. Repeat with remaining crepes and filling.

  Bake, covered, in a 350° oven for 20 minutes. Reheat remaining sauce; pour some atop crepes. Sprinkle crepes with the remaining 1 cup cheese. Pass remaining sauce. Garnish with fresh hot peppers and cherry tomatoes. Serves 4.

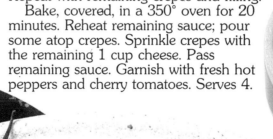

# Bulgur and Sausage-Stuffed Turkey Thighs

| | |
|---|---|
| **2 fresh *or* frozen turkey thighs** | ● Thaw turkey thighs, if frozen. |
| **⅓ cup bulgur wheat** <br> **⅔ cup hot water** | ● Meanwhile, soak bulgur in hot water for 1 hour. Drain well; squeeze out excess water. |
| **½ pound bulk pork sausage** <br> **½ cup chopped onion** | ● In skillet cook sausage and onion till meat is brown; drain. |
| **1 4-ounce can chopped mushrooms, drained** <br> **½ cup chopped tart apple** <br> **½ cup chopped walnuts** <br> **2 tablespoons snipped parsley** <br> **¼ teaspoon dried thyme, crushed** <br> **⅛ teaspoon salt** <br> **⅛ teaspoon pepper** <br> **1 beaten egg** | ● Add the drained bulgur, the chopped mushrooms, the chopped apple, the chopped walnuts, the snipped parsley, the crushed dried thyme, the salt, and the pepper. Stir in the beaten egg. |

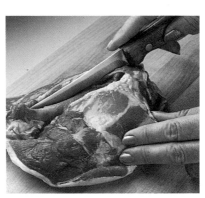

**To debone turkey thighs, use a sharp boning knife. Carefully cut meat along one side of the bone.**

● Debone the turkey thighs. Pound thighs to ½-inch thickness. With skin side down, spoon *half* of the stuffing over *each* thigh. Roll up, jelly-roll style, starting at narrow end. Secure the rolls with string.

Place thighs in a shallow baking pan. Bake, covered, in a 350° oven 1 hour. Uncover and bake 45 minutes more or till done. Makes 6 to 8 servings.

**Gently pull meat away from the bone.**

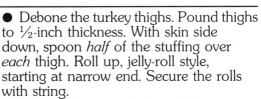

# Chicken and Grains Soup

| | |
|---|---|
| 6 **chicken thighs** <br> 6 **small chicken legs** <br> 2 **tablespoons cooking oil** | ● In a large saucepan or Dutch oven brown half of the chicken thighs and legs at a time in hot oil over medium heat about 15 minutes. Remove chicken. Drain fat, if necessary. |
| 7 **cups chicken broth** <br> 1 **cup pearl barley** *or* **regular brown rice** <br> ½ **cup wheat berries** *or* **millet** <br> 1 **medium onion, chopped** <br> 2 **bay leaves** <br> ¼ **teaspoon pepper** | ● To saucepan add chicken broth, barley or brown rice, wheat berries or millet, onion, bay leaves, and pepper. Bring mixture to boiling; reduce heat. Return chicken to pan. Simmer, covered, over medium heat for 30 minutes. |
| 4 **medium carrots, bias-sliced into ½-inch pieces** <br> 1 **9-ounce package frozen cut green beans, thawed** <br> 3 **stalks celery, bias-sliced into ½-inch pieces** | ● Stir in bias-sliced carrots, thawed cut green beans, and bias-sliced celery. Cook, covered, about 15 minutes more or till chicken and grains are tender. Remove and discard bay leaves. |
| 1 **8-ounce package cream cheese, cubed** <br> **Snipped parsley** | ● Stir in cream cheese; cook and stir till cheese melts. Garnish with parsley, if desired. Makes 8 servings. |

**This creamy, chunky soup is just perfect as a stick-to-the-ribs main course on a cold winter day. Serve it in soup plates rather than bowls so guests can really dig in with knives, forks, and spoons.**

# Couscous Chicken Rolls

| | |
|---|---|
| ¼ cup boiling water<br>¼ cup ready-to-cook couscous | ● In a bowl pour boiling water over couscous; let stand 5 minutes. |
| 4 whole large chicken breasts, skinned, halved lengthwise, and boned | ● Meanwhile, place one piece of chicken between two pieces of clear plastic wrap. Working from center to edges, pound chicken lightly with a meat mallet, forming a rectangle about ⅛ inch thick. Remove plastic wrap. Repeat with the remaining chicken pieces. |
| ¼ cup dried currants *or* chopped raisins<br>3 tablespoons dairy sour cream<br>3 tablespoons sliced green onion<br>½ teaspoon grated gingerroot *or* ⅛ teaspoon ground ginger<br>¼ teaspoon salt | ● Add currants or chopped raisins, sour cream, sliced green onion, gingerroot or ground ginger, and salt to couscous.<br>  Place about *2 tablespoons* of the couscous mixture on each chicken piece. Fold in sides; roll up jelly-roll style, pressing all edges together gently with your fingers to seal. Secure chicken rolls with a wooden pick. |
| 3 tablespoons butter *or* margarine<br>2 tablespoons honey<br>1 tablespoon soy sauce | ● In skillet heat butter or margarine. Fry chicken rolls on all sides about 5 minutes or till brown. Simmer, covered, for 10 to 15 minutes or till nearly done. Combine the honey and soy sauce; pour over rolls. Cook, covered, 5 minutes more, spooning juices over the chicken rolls. Makes 4 servings. |

**Although couscous (semolina) may sound exotic, it is really a farina-like by-product of durum wheat. You can buy this traditional native food of the Middle East and North Africa in many larger American grocery stores. Use it to add an ethnic touch to everyday meals.**

# Shrimp with Millet

1 pound fresh *or* frozen shelled shrimp
⅔ cup millet
¼ cup sliced green onion
2 tablespoons butter *or* margarine

● Thaw shrimp, if frozen; devein shrimp. Halve large shrimp lengthwise. In a large saucepan cook the millet and green onion in butter or margarine till lightly browned and onion is tender.

---

1½ cups chicken broth
¼ teaspoon ground pepper
⅓ cup cashews

● Stir in chicken broth and pepper. Bring to boiling; reduce heat. Simmer, covered, for 15 minutes. Remove from heat. Stir in cashews. Keep warm while stir-frying shrimp.

---

3 tablespoons soy sauce
2 teaspoons cornstarch
3 tablespoons dry sherry
1 teaspoon grated gingerroot
1 teaspoon sugar
⅛ to ¼ teaspoon crushed red pepper
2 tablespoons cooking oil
1 cup sliced fresh mushrooms
1 6-ounce package frozen pea pods, thawed
1 medium tomato, peeled, seeded, and chopped
Whole fresh mushrooms (optional)

● Stir soy sauce into cornstarch; stir in dry sherry, gingerroot, sugar, and red pepper. Set aside.
  Preheat a wok or large skillet over high heat; add cooking oil. Stir-fry sliced mushrooms in hot oil 1 to 2 minutes or till crisp-tender. Remove from wok. Add more oil, if necessary. Add shrimp to hot wok or skillet; stir-fry 1 to 2 minutes or till shrimp are done. Push shrimp away from center of wok or skillet.
  Stir soy sauce mixture and add to center of wok or skillet. Cook and stir till thickened and bubbly. Stir in cooked mushrooms, pea pods, and tomato. Cover and cook 1 minute. Serve over millet mixture. Garnish with whole mushrooms, if desired. Serves 4.

To transform a plain mushroom into a fancy garnish like the one below, use a punch-type can opener to make indentations on the mushroom cap.

# Wheat Berry Waldorf

½ cup vanilla yogurt
2 tablespoons mayonnaise
  *or* salad dressing
⅛ teaspoon salt
1 cup cooked wheat berries
  (see cooking directions,
  page 8)
½ cup thinly sliced celery

● Stir together the vanilla yogurt, the mayonnaise or salad dressing, and the salt. Add the cooked wheat berries and the thinly sliced celery.
  Cover and chill 1 hour, if desired.

Lettuce leaves
2 medium apples, cored and
  sliced

● To serve, place lettuce leaves on individual serving plates. Arrange apple slices atop lettuce. Spoon wheat berry mixture atop. Makes 4 servings.

**If you're in a hurry or want to serve this unusual salad for a buffet, chop up the apples and mix all the ingredients together as you would for a traditional Waldorf salad. Line your prettiest bowl with lettuce, add the salad, and let everyone help himself.**

# Bulgur-Cabbage Salad

2 cups warm water
1 cup bulgur wheat

● In a mixing bowl combine the warm water and bulgur; let stand 1 hour. Drain bulgur well, pressing out excess water.

2 cups coarsely shredded
    green *or* red cabbage
1 cup frozen peas, thawed
1 cup chopped tomato
¼ cup olive *or* salad oil
¼ cup lemon juice
¼ teaspoon dried dillweed
  Lettuce leaves

● Stir in the shredded cabbage and the peas. Stir together the chopped tomato, olive oil or salad oil, lemon juice, and the dried dillweed. Stir tomato mixture into bulgur-cabbage mixture.
  Cover and chill till serving time. To serve, spoon the salad into a lettuce-lined bowl. Makes 8 servings.

**Just set out Bulgur-Cabbage Salad at your next barbecue alongside the burgers or steaks. That's about all you'll need for dinner since this dish doubles as both a vegetable and a salad.**

# Pasta and Millet Salad

| | |
|---|---|
| 8 cups water<br>⅓ cup millet<br>1 teaspoon salt<br>4 ounces rosamarina *or* acini di pepe (⅔ cup) | ● In large saucepan combine water, millet, and salt. Bring to boiling. Cook for 8 minutes; add rosamarina or acini di pepe. Cook 5 minutes more. Drain in colander. Rinse with cold water. Drain. |
| ¼ cup salad oil<br>¼ cup white wine vinegar<br>1 teaspoon sugar<br>1 teaspoon fines herbes<br>½ cup thinly sliced green onion | ● For dressing, combine salad oil, white wine vinegar, sugar, and fines herbes. Combine pasta-millet mixture, dressing, and green onion. Chill salad several hours or overnight. |
| ½ cup thinly sliced red radish, quartered | ● To serve, combine chilled pasta-millet mixture and radish. Toss to mix well. Makes 6 servings. |

**Petite pasta—that's the best way to describe rosamarina and acini di pepe. You'll find them at Italian specialty shops.**

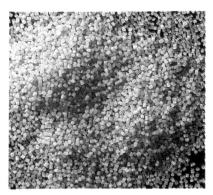

**Acini di pepe**

**Rosamarina**

# Tabouleh

| 1 cup bulgur wheat | ● Place bulgur in colander. Rinse with cold water. Drain well. |
|---|---|
| 2 cups snipped parsley<br>1 large cucumber, finely chopped<br>½ cup finely chopped green onion | ● In a large bowl combine the drained bulgur, the snipped parsley, the finely chopped cucumber, and the finely chopped green onion. |
| ⅓ cup cooking oil<br>⅓ cup lemon juice<br>1 tablespoon snipped fresh mint<br>½ teaspoon salt<br>⅛ teaspoon pepper<br>1 clove garlic, minced | ● For dressing, in a screw-top jar combine cooking oil, lemon juice, mint, salt, pepper, and garlic; shake to mix. Add to bulgur mixture. Toss gently till well coated. Cover and chill overnight. |
| 1 large tomato, chopped<br>Chopped cucumber (optional) | ● Before serving, stir in tomato and additional cucumber, if desired. Garnish with tomato rose, cucumber flowers, and fresh mint, if desired (see tip, opposite). Makes 6 to 8 servings. |

**Tabouleh is a Middle Eastern favorite, but each country has its own distinctive way of serving this refreshing salad. This version is Jordanian with its abundance of fresh parsley. Import Tabouleh to your next all-American beach party or picnic.**

# Barley Salad

|  |  |
|---|---|
| 1 cup pearl barley<br>3 cups water, chicken, *or* beef broth | ● Cook barley in boiling salted water or broth till tender, about 1 hour. Drain and rinse with cold water. Drain well. |
| 1 cup cooked *or* canned garbanzo beans, drained<br>½ to 1 cup cashews<br>½ cup shredded carrot<br>¼ cup snipped parsley *or* coriander<br>2 tablespoons fresh mint *or* 2 teaspoons dried mint | ● In a large mixing bowl stir together the drained barley, the garbanzo beans, the cashews, the shredded carrot, the snipped parsley or coriander, and the fresh or dried mint. |
| 3 tablespoons cooking oil<br>3 tablespoons lemon juice<br>¼ teaspoon salt<br>¼ teaspoon pepper | ● Combine the cooking oil, the lemon juice, the salt, and the pepper; pour over the barley mixture and toss to coat. Chill for several hours. |
| Lettuce leaves<br>Parsley (optional)<br>Carrot curls (optional) | ● Arrange lettuce leaves in a salad bowl. Turn salad mixture into the bowl. Garnish with parsley and carrot curls, if desired. Makes 8 servings. |

**In a hurry? You can speed the preparation time for this salad by starting with quick-cooking barley. Substitute 1⅔ cups quick-cooking barley for the pearl barley and use 2¼ cups water or broth. You'll have to boil the mixture only 10 to 12 minutes instead of an hour.**

# Easy Salad Garnish

All you need are a few mint leaves, a tomato, and a cucumber to fashion the sophisticated vegetable flower garnish pictured *opposite*. To make the tomato rose, start with a medium-size ripe tomato. Cut a "base" from the stem end of the tomato (do not sever). Continue cutting one continuous narrow strip (¾ inch wide) of tomato in a spiral fashion, using a sawing motion, and tapering the end into a point. Curl the strip onto its base in the shape of an opening rose; use remaining tomato for another use.
To make the cucumber flowers, thinly slice 1 medium cucumber. Soak slices in salted ice water for 5 minutes. Drain slices. Tightly roll up a small cucumber slice. Continue wrapping slices around the first slice, using about 4 slices for each flower. Secure with a wooden pick at one end. Fold out ends of cucumber slices to resemble a flower.

# Barley-Stuffed Peppers

| | | |
|---|---|---|
| 4 large green peppers | ● Cut green peppers in half lengthwise; remove seeds and membranes. If desired, precook pepper halves in boiling salted *water* for 3 minutes; drain. | **Barley-Stuffed Peppers are a twist on the traditional stuffed pepper. Peppers are halved lengthwise and served open-face with a barley-vegetable-cheese filling. Cooked pearl barley or quick-cooking barley works equally well.** |

| | |
|---|---|
| 1 beaten egg<br>⅓ cup soft bread crumbs<br>1 cup shredded Monterey Jack cheese with jalapeño peppers<br>1 large tomato, peeled, seeded, and chopped<br>½ cup shredded zucchini<br>1 4-ounce can chopped mushrooms, drained<br>¼ cup toasted sesame seed<br>1 teaspoon onion salt<br>1½ cups cooked barley *or* cooked brown rice (see cooking directions, page 9) | ● Stir together the egg, the soft bread crumbs, ¾ *cup* of the cheese, the chopped tomato, the shredded zucchini, the chopped mushrooms, the toasted sesame seed, the onion salt, and the cooked barley or brown rice. Divide evenly among pepper halves.<br>    Sprinkle the remaining cheese atop filling. Place peppers in a 13x9x2-inch baking pan.<br>    Bake peppers in a 350° oven for 25 to 30 minutes or till heated through. Makes 8 servings. |

# Storing Whole Grains

Because whole grain products contain the oil-rich germ that can easily become rancid, it's best to buy them in small quantities. Store them up to 5 months, tightly covered, in a cool, dry place. For longer storage, refrigerate or freeze grains, tightly covered, in moisture- and vaporproof containers. Before adding refrigerated whole grain flour in yeast bread recipes, warm the flour to room temperature.

# Corn-Oat Scallop

1 beaten egg
1 cup milk
½ cup toasted rolled oats
  (see tip, below)
¼ teaspoon salt
⅛ teaspoon pepper

● In a bowl stir together the beaten egg, the milk, the toasted rolled oats, the salt, and the pepper.

1 8¾-ounce can whole
  kernel corn, drained
1 8½-ounce can cream-style
  corn
¼ cup sliced green onion

● Stir in corn and onion. Turn into an 8x1½-inch round baking dish.
  Bake in a 350° oven for 30 to 35 minutes. Let stand 5 minutes before serving. Makes 6 servings.

Once you've made scalloped corn with toasted rolled oats, you may never again want to use standard recipes that call for bread or cracker crumbs. The oats are more than just filler: They add a delicate nutty flavor to this family favorite.

# Toasted Rolled Oats

To make toasted rolled oats, place ½ cup quick-cooking or regular rolled oats in a shallow baking pan. Bake in a 350° oven for 15 to 20 minutes or till oats are lightly browned. Cool. (Note: A counter-top toaster oven is the perfect size for toasting small amounts of rolled oats.)

# Pick-a-Flavor Pasta

1⅓ cups all-purpose flour
 1 cup whole wheat *or* rye flour
 1 teaspoon dried basil, crushed; dried marjoram, crushed; *or* dried sage, crushed; *or* 2 teaspoons curry powder *or* chili powder
 ½ teaspoon salt

● In a bowl stir together the all-purpose flour, ½ *cup* of the whole wheat or rye flour, desired seasoning, and salt. Make a well in the center of the dry ingredients.

2 beaten eggs
⅓ cup water
 1 teaspoon cooking oil

● Combine eggs, water, and oil. Add to the dry ingredients; mix well. Turn dough out onto surface sprinkled with some of the remaining whole wheat or rye flour; knead till smooth and elastic (8 to 10 minutes total), adding flour as needed. Cover; let rest 10 minutes.

● Divide dough into thirds. On a floured surface roll each portion into a 16x12-inch rectangle. *Or,* if using a pasta machine, pass dough through the machine till 1/16 inch thick. Let dough stand, uncovered, 20 minutes.

● To cut dough by hand, roll up loosely. Cut into ¼-inch-wide slices; unroll. Lift and shake to separate into strips. To cut using a pasta machine, pass dough through a ¼-inch-wide cutting blade. Cut strips into desired lengths. Follow tips for cooking or drying, *opposite*. Makes 1 pound fresh pasta.

# Cooking Pasta

To cook fresh pasta, in a large kettle or Dutch oven combine 3 quarts *water* and 1 tablespoon *salt.* Bring to a rolling boil. If desired, add 1 tablespoon *cooking oil* to help keep pasta separated. Add 8 ounces *pasta.* Cook, uncovered, about 2 minutes. Drain pasta and serve immediately with your favorite sauce. Or, for a quick and easy, cheesy side dish, toss the hot cooked pasta with ¼ cup *butter* or *margarine,* melted, and ¼ cup *grated Parmesan cheese.* Makes 8 servings.

A pound of fresh pasta may be more than you need for one meal. Dry the extra on a pasta drying rack or on a coat hanger. Let the pasta stand overnight or till completely dry. Wrap in clear plastic wrap or foil or place in an airtight container. Store in a dry place. For freezer storage, let cut pasta dry at least 1 hour. Wrap in moisture- and vaporproof wrap and freeze for up to 8 months.

# Herbed Kasha Pilaf

| ½ cup chopped onion<br>1 tablespoon butter *or* margarine | ● In a 2-quart saucepan cook onion in butter or margarine till onion is tender but not brown. |

| 1½ cups water<br>1½ teaspoons instant chicken bouillon granules<br>½ teaspoon dried basil, crushed<br>⅓ cup long grain rice | ● Add water, instant chicken bouillon granules, and basil. Bring to boiling; add rice. Reduce heat. Simmer, covered, for 10 minutes. |

| 1 beaten egg<br>⅓ cup coarsely ground roasted buckwheat groats (kasha)<br>2 tablespoons snipped parsley | ● Meanwhile, in a bowl stir together the egg and buckwheat groats. Stir into rice. Simmer, covered, for 10 minutes longer or till groats and rice are tender. Stir in the snipped parsley. Makes 4 servings. |

**Surprised to see egg in this pilaf recipe? You'll see the egg in the finished dish, too, because the egg coats the buckwheat grains so they remain separate. It's almost like eating Chinese fried rice.**

# Cheesy Brown Rice Balls with Vegetable Sauce

| | |
|---|---|
| **3 beaten eggs**<br>**3 cups cooked brown rice, cooled (see cooking directions, page 9)**<br>**⅔ cup all-purpose flour**<br>**½ teaspoon salt**<br>**¼ teaspoon pepper** | ● In bowl stir together the beaten eggs, the cooked brown rice, the ⅔ cup all-purpose flour, ½ teaspoon salt, and the ¼ teaspoon pepper. |
| **3 ounces American cheese**<br>**⅔ cup crushed saltine crackers** | ● Cut the cheese into thirty-six ½-inch cubes. Set aside 12 cheese cubes. With wet hands shape about 2 tablespoons of the rice mixture around a cheese cube. Repeat with remaining rice and cheese cubes to make 24 rice balls. Roll rice balls in cracker crumbs. |
| **Cooking oil** | ● In an 8-inch skillet add cooking oil to ½-inch depth; heat. Fry rice balls, 4 or 5 at a time, in hot oil (365°) about 2½ to 3 minutes or till golden, turning once. Drain on paper toweling; keep warm. |
| **2 tablespoons chopped green pepper**<br>**2 tablespoons chopped onion**<br>**2 tablespoons shredded carrot**<br>**2 tablespoons butter *or* margarine**<br>**2 tablespoons all-purpose flour**<br>**½ teaspoon salt**<br>**Dash pepper**<br>**1¼ cups milk** | ● For vegetable sauce, in small saucepan cook green pepper, onion, and carrot in butter or margarine till tender but not brown. Add 2 tablespoons flour, ½ teaspoon salt, and dash pepper.<br>　Add milk all at once. Cook and stir till thickened; cook 1 minute more. Add reserved cheese cubes, stirring till melted. To serve, pour vegetable sauce over rice balls. Makes 6 to 8 servings. |

**To shape rice balls, wet hands and form about 2 tablespoons of the rice mixture into a ball around each ½-inch cheese cube.**

**Fry rice balls, 4 or 5 at a time, in hot cooking oil (365°) for 2½ to 3 minutes or till golden brown. Drain on paper toweling. Keep warm.**

# Crunchy Brown Rice Snacks

| | |
|---|---|
| 1½  cups regular brown rice<br>1½  teaspoons seasoned salt | ● Cook rice according to directions on page 9, *except* add seasoned salt to water. Cool rice thoroughly.<br>    Pat rice into a well-greased 15x10x1-inch baking pan. Bake in a 300° oven for 1½ hours or till rice is dried. Turn out of baking pan; cool. Break into approximately 3x1-inch pieces. |
| ¼  cup cooking oil | ● In a heavy skillet heat oil over medium heat till a kernel of uncooked rice sizzles in the oil. Add rice pieces, a few at a time. Cook over medium heat for 30 to 45 seconds per side or till light golden brown. Add more oil, if necessary. Drain on paper toweling. |
| **Grated Parmesan cheese (optional)** | ● Lightly sprinkle with Parmesan cheese, if desired. Store in a tightly covered container. Makes about 48. |

**Turn rice out of pan. Cool and break into 3x1-inch pieces.**

**Sprinkle fried rice pieces with grated Parmesan cheese, if desired.**

# Homemade-Cereal Snack Mix

| | |
|---|---|
| 2 cups Wheat Cereal *or* Bran Cereal (see recipes, pages 10 and 11)* | ● In a mixing bowl stir together the Wheat or Bran Cereal, the dry roasted peanuts, the coconut chips, the shelled pumpkin seed, the ground cinnamon, and the ground nutmeg. |
| 1 cup dry roasted peanuts | |
| ½ cup coconut chips | |
| ⅓ cup shelled pumpkin seed | |
| ½ teaspoon ground cinnamon | |
| ¼ teaspoon ground nutmeg | |
| ¼ cup honey | ● Combine honey and butter. Stir into cereal mixture. Spread in a 13x9x2-inch baking pan. Bake in a 375° oven for 10 to 15 minutes, stirring twice. Store in an airtight container in a cool place or in refrigerator. Makes 4 cups. |
| ¼ cup butter *or* margarine, melted | |

*Note: If you prefer, substitute 2 cups bite-size shredded wheat or bran squares for Wheat Cereal or Bran Cereal.

**Sweet munching is what you get when you make Homemade-Cereal Snack Mix. Use your imagination to cut the homemade cereals into a variety of shapes. (We show you two possibilities on page 10.) If you're in too much of a hurry to start from scratch, you can substitue ready-made cereal.**

# Refrigerator Whole Wheat Chippers

| | |
|---|---|
| 2⅔ cups whole wheat flour<br>1 teaspoon baking soda<br>½ teaspoon ground cinnamon<br>½ teaspoon salt | ● In a bowl stir together the whole wheat flour, the baking soda, the ground cinnamon, and the salt. |
| 1 cup shortening<br>½ cup packed brown sugar<br>⅓ cup honey | ● In a mixer bowl beat shortening on medium speed of electric mixer for 30 seconds. Add brown sugar and honey. Beat till fluffy. |
| 1 egg<br>1 teaspoon vanilla | ● Add egg and vanilla; beat well. Add dry ingredients to beaten mixture and beat till well blended. |
| 1 cup miniature semisweet chocolate pieces | ● Stir in the miniature chocolate pieces. Cover and chill dough about 45 minutes for easier handling. |
| ¼ cup toasted wheat germ | ● Shape into two 8-inch-long rolls; roll in wheat germ to coat surface. Wrap in waxed paper or clear plastic wrap; chill at least 6 hours. |
| | ● Cut dough into ¼-inch slices. Place 1 inch apart on a greased cookie sheet. Bake in a 375° oven for 10 to 15 minutes or till done. Cool about 1 minute before removing to wire rack; cool. Makes about 60 cookies. |

**Anytime you want a fresh chocolate chip cookie, you can have it—thanks to this refrigerator whole wheat version. Slice as many cookies as you want to bake at a time. Be sure to use mini-chocolate chips; they're a must for easy slicing of the chilled cookie dough.**

**The dough will keep for a week in the refrigerator. Or, you can wrap the rolls in moisture- and vaporproof wrap and store them in the freezer for up to a month.**

# Chewy Honey-Granola Bars

½ cup packed brown sugar
½ cup butter *or* margarine
⅓ cup honey

● In a saucepan combine brown sugar, butter or margarine, and honey. Bring to boiling, stirring constantly.

5 cups Good-for-You Granola (see recipe, page 12)
½ cup whole wheat flour

● Stir together granola and whole wheat flour. Pour brown sugar mixture over granola mixture. Stir till granola mixture is well coated. Press mixture into a greased 13x9x2 inch baking pan. Cool; cut into bars. Makes 24 bars.

# Peanut and Rice Drops

¾ **cup all-purpose flour**
½ **cup brown rice flour (see tip, page 19)**
¾ **teaspoon baking soda**

● In a bowl stir together the all-purpose flour, the brown rice flour, and the baking soda.

½ **cup butter** *or* **margarine**
½ **cup peanut butter**
½ **cup packed brown sugar**
½ **cup sugar**

● In mixer bowl beat butter and peanut butter on medium speed of electric mixer for 30 seconds. Add brown sugar and sugar; beat till fluffy.

1 **egg**
½ **teaspoon vanilla**
1 **cup chopped salted peanuts**

● Add egg and vanilla; beat well. Add dry ingredients to beaten mixture and beat till well blended. Stir in chopped salted peanuts.

● Drop dough by rounded teaspoons about 2 inches apart onto an ungreased cookie sheet. Bake in a 375° oven about 10 minutes or till done. Remove from cookie sheet; cool on wire rack. Makes about 42 cookies.

**If you like crunchy cookies, then try these double-peanut pleasers. It's the brown rice flour that makes the cookies crispy. Grind your own flour (see directions, page 19) or purchase brown rice flour.**

# Cracked Wheat Cookies

| | | |
|---|---|---|
| 1½ cups all-purpose flour<br>¼ teaspoon ground<br>    cardamom<br>¼ teaspoon salt | ● In a bowl stir together all-purpose flour, ground cardamom, and salt. | **Cracked wheat takes the place of nuts in these cookies, adding fiber and flavor. Try it in other cookies, too.** |
| ⅔ cup butter *or* margarine<br>⅔ cup sugar<br>1 tablespoon milk | ● In mixer bowl beat butter or margarine on medium speed of electric mixer for 30 seconds. Add sugar and beat till fluffy. Add milk; beat well. Add dry ingredients and beat till well blended. | |
| ½ cup cooked cracked wheat<br>   *or* cooked steel-cut oats<br>   (**see cooking directions,**<br>   **page 8**)<br>¼ cup finely chopped<br>   maraschino cherries<br>   **Sugar** | ● Stir in cooked cracked wheat or steel-cut oats and cherries. Drop by rounded teaspoonfuls onto ungreased cookie sheet. Dip tines of fork in sugar; flatten cookies using sugar-coated fork, first in one direction, then the opposite. Bake in a 375° oven for 10 to 12 minutes or till done. Remove to wire rack; cool. Makes about 36 cookies. | |

# Double-Wheat Cookies

| | | |
|---|---|---|
| 1 cup butter *or* margarine,<br>   softened<br>½ cup packed brown sugar<br>¼ cup toasted wheat germ<br>1¾ cups whole wheat flour | ● In large mixer bowl cream together butter or margarine, brown sugar, and the ¼ cup wheat germ till light and fluffy. Stir in whole wheat flour. | **These whole grain cookies are so buttery rich and yummy, you'll want to make them often.** |
| **Toasted wheat germ** | ● Form into 1-inch balls. Roll in additional wheat germ. Place on an ungreased cookie sheet; flatten with tines of fork.<br>   Bake in a 350° oven for 10 to 12 minutes. Remove from cookie sheet. Cool on wire rack. Makes 36 cookies. | |

# Double-Wheat Foldovers

½ cup cooked wheat berries (see cooking directions, page 8)
2 tablespoons raspberry jam

● For filling, combine cooked wheat berries and raspberry jam. Cover; chill.

1½ cups whole wheat flour
1 teaspoon baking powder
¼ teaspoon salt

● Stir together the whole wheat flour, baking powder, and salt.

½ cup butter *or* margarine
½ cup packed brown sugar

● In mixer bowl beat butter on medium speed of electric mixer for 30 seconds. Add sugar; beat till fluffy.

1 egg
1 teaspoon vanilla
Powdered Sugar Icing (see recipe, page 87)

● Add egg and vanilla; beat well. Add dry ingredients; beat till well blended. Cover; chill for 2 hours. On lightly floured surface roll dough to ⅛-inch thickness. Cut with 2½-inch-round cutter. Place about *1 teaspoon* filling in center of each dough circle. Fold dough in half over filling; seal edges using fork tines. Place on an ungreased cookie sheet. Bake in a 375° oven for 10 to 12 minutes. Cool on wire rack. Drizzle with Powdered Sugar Icing. Makes 24.

Cookie snitchers have a hard time keeping away from Double-Wheat Foldovers. They just love these crispy cookies with the chewy surprise inside. We combined raspberry jam with wheat berries for the filling; you can use any jam flavor you like.

# Mocha-Oatmeal Cupcakes

| | |
|---|---|
| ½ cup hot water<br>½ cup quick-cooking rolled oats<br>1 5½-ounce can chocolate-flavored syrup<br>¼ cup butter *or* margarine<br>1 teaspoon instant coffee crystals<br>1 teaspoon vanilla | ● In a mixing bowl pour hot water over oats. Add the chocolate-flavored syrup, butter or margarine, instant coffee crystals, and vanilla. Let oatmeal mixture stand 10 minutes; stir till well combined. |
| ⅔ cup all-purpose flour<br>⅓ cup sugar<br>½ teaspoon baking soda<br>¼ teaspoon salt | ● In mixer bowl stir together the flour, sugar, baking soda, and salt. |
| 2 eggs<br>⅓ cup chopped nuts | ● Add eggs and oatmeal mixture; beat on low speed of electric mixer till well combined. Stir in nuts. Line muffin pan with paper bake cups; fill ¾ full. |
| Coffee Cream Icing | ● Bake cupcakes in a 375° oven for 20 to 25 minutes or till a wooden pick inserted in center comes out clean. Cool on wire rack. Frost with Coffee Cream Icing. Makes 12 cupcakes. |
| | ● **Coffee Cream Icing:** In a small mixer bowl beat ¾ cup sifted *powdered sugar* and ¼ cup *butter* or *margarine* with an electric mixer till fluffy. Dissolve 1 teaspoon *instant coffee crystals* in 1 tablespoon *milk* and ½ teaspoon *vanilla*. Beat into sugar-butter mixture. Gradually beat in an additional 1 cup sifted *powdered sugar*. If necessary, add additional *milk* to make of spreading consistency. Makes 1 cup. |

Coffee flavor—inside and out—is what you get in these fudgy cupcakes. You won't be able to see or taste the rolled oats, but you'll notice the texture they add to the cupcakes.

# Wild Rice Cake

²⁄₃ cup wild rice

● Cook rice according to cooking directions on page 9, *except* cook 5 minutes longer. Drain, cover, and chill.

**Powdered Sugar Icing:** Stir together 1 cup sifted *powdered sugar* and ¼ teaspoon *vanilla*. Add enough *milk* or *brandy* to make of drizzling consistency (about 1½ tablespoons).

2 cups whole wheat flour
1 cup all-purpose flour
2 teaspoons baking soda
½ teaspoon salt
¼ teaspoon ground nutmeg
   *or* cardamom

● Grease and lightly flour a 10-inch fluted tube pan. In a bowl stir together the whole wheat flour, the all-purpose flour, the baking soda, the salt, and the ground nutmeg or the cardamom.

1 cup butter *or* margarine
1 cup packed brown sugar
1 teaspoon vanilla

● In mixer bowl beat butter or margarine on medium speed of electric mixer for 30 seconds. Add brown sugar and vanilla; beat till fluffy.

5 eggs
1 cup buttermilk
   Powdered Sugar Icing
   (see recipe, right)

● Add eggs, one at a time, beating 1 minute after each; batter will look curdled. Add dry ingredients and buttermilk alternately to beaten mixture, beating after each addition. Stir in rice. Turn out into prepared pan. Bake in a 350° oven for 50 to 55 minutes or till done. Cool for 15 minutes on wire rack. Remove from pan; cool. Frost with Powdered Sugar Icing. Serves 12.

# Bran-Banana Cake

| 1½ cups all-purpose flour *or* whole wheat flour<br>½ cup unprocessed wheat bran<br>1½ teaspoons baking powder<br>¼ teaspoon salt<br>¼ teaspoon ground allspice | ● In a bowl stir together the all-purpose or whole wheat flour, the unprocessed wheat bran, the baking powder, the salt, and the ground allspice. | **Good as cake, but good as cookies, too. To make Bran-Banana Bars, turn batter into a greased 15x10x1-inch baking pan. Bake in a 350° oven for 20 to 25 minutes. Leave unfrosted for snacking.** |
| --- | --- | --- |
| 2 eggs<br>¾ cup packed brown sugar<br>⅔ cup cooking oil<br>1 teaspoon vanilla | ● In a bowl stir together the eggs, brown sugar, cooking oil, and vanilla; beat till well blended. | |
| 1 cup mashed banana (3 medium)<br>½ cup chopped nuts<br>Cream Cheese Frosting | ● Stir mashed bananas into egg mixture. Stir dry ingredients and nuts into banana mixture. Spread in a greased 13x9x2-inch baking pan. Bake in a 350° oven for 25 to 30 minutes or till done. Cool in pan on wire rack. Frost with Cream Cheese Frosting. Cover; store in the refrigerator. Serves 12 to 15. | |
| | **Cream Cheese Frosting:** In a mixer bowl beat one 3-ounce package *cream cheese,* softened; ¼ cup *butter or margarine,* softened; and 1 teaspoon *vanilla* till light and fluffy. Gradually add 2 cups sifted *powdered sugar;* beat till frosting is smooth. | |

# Yogurt-Rhubarb Cake

|  |  |
|---|---|
| 2 tablespoons butter *or* margarine, melted<br>½ cup packed brown sugar<br>½ cup chopped pecans<br>¼ cup all-purpose flour<br>1 teaspoon ground cinnamon | ● For topping, in a small bowl combine the 2 tablespoons melted butter or margarine, the ½ cup brown sugar, pecans, ¼ cup all-purpose flour, and 1 teaspoon cinnamon. Set aside. |
| 1 cup whole wheat flour<br>1 cup all-purpose flour<br>1½ teaspoons baking powder<br>1 teaspoon ground cinnamon<br>½ teaspoon baking soda<br>½ teaspoon salt | ● For cake, in a medium mixing bowl stir together the whole wheat flour, the 1 cup all-purpose flour, baking powder, 1 teaspoon ground cinnamon, baking soda, and salt. Set aside. |
| 1 8-ounce carton cherry-vanilla yogurt<br>3 tablespoons milk | ● In a small bowl combine the cherry-vanilla yogurt and milk. |
| 1 cup packed brown sugar<br>½ cup butter *or* margarine<br>2 eggs<br>1 teaspoon vanilla | ● In large mixer bowl beat together the 1 cup brown sugar and the ½ cup butter or margarine. Add eggs and vanilla; beat till fluffy.<br><br>Alternately add the whole wheat flour mixture and the yogurt mixture to the egg mixture, beating till well blended. |
| 2½ cups chopped fresh rhubarb *or* frozen rhubarb, thawed | ● Fold in rhubarb. Pour batter into a greased and floured 13x9x2-inch baking pan. Sprinkle topping over butter. Bake in a 350° oven for 45 to 50 minutes or till done. Cool in pan on wire rack. Serve warm or cool. Makes 15 servings. |

**Don't limit yourself to using cherry-vanilla yogurt in this cake. We tried strawberry yogurt and liked it, too. You might want to experiment with other flavors. But if you can't find a flavor you like, plain yogurt works just fine.**

# Whole Wheat-Fruit Shortcake

| | |
|---|---|
| 1 | cup all-purpose flour |
| ¾ | cup whole wheat *or* triticale flour |
| ¼ | cup sugar |
| 1 | tablespoon baking powder |
| ¼ | teaspoon salt |
| ¼ | teaspoon ground nutmeg |
| ⅛ | teaspoon ground ginger |
| ½ | cup butter *or* margarine |
| 1 | beaten egg |
| ⅔ | cup milk |
| ¾ | cup cooked wheat berries (see cooking directions, page 9) |

● In a mixing bowl stir together all-purpose flour, whole wheat or triticale flour, sugar, baking powder, salt, nutmeg, and ginger. Cut in butter or margarine till mixture resembles coarse crumbs.

Combine beaten egg and milk. Add all at once to flour mixture. Add wheat berries, stirring just till moistened. Spread dough in two greased 8x1½-inch round baking pans.

Bake in a 450° oven for 10 to 12 minutes or till done. Cool shortcake in pans for 10 minutes. Remove from pans; cool on wire rack.

**Cream Filling:**
In a small mixer bowl beat one 3-ounce package softened *cream cheese* till smooth and fluffy. Add one 8-ounce carton *vanilla yogurt;* beat at low speed till well combined. Cover and chill. Makes 1¼ cups.

| | |
|---|---|
| 3 | cups fresh fruit |
| | Lemon juice (optional) |
| | Cream Filling (see recipe, right) |
| | Honey (optional) |

● Slice or halve fruit as desired. If using bananas, pears, peaches, or apples, dip slices in lemon juice to prevent browning.

Place one of the shortcake layers on a serving plate, flat side up. Spread *half* of the Cream Filling atop layer. Arrange *half* of the sliced fruit atop filling. Place the top layer of shortcake on the fruit, rounded side up. Top with the remaining filling and fruit. Drizzle honey atop shortcake, if desired. Cut into wedges to serve. Makes 8 servings.

# Pearadise Pie

3½ **cups flaked whole grain cereal**
¼ **cup toasted wheat germ**
6 **tablespoons butter or margarine, melted**

● For crust, place cereal in a plastic bag or between 2 sheets of waxed paper. Crush into fine crumbs; measure *1¼ cups* crumbs.

Place crumbs in medium mixing bowl; stir in wheat germ and melted butter or margarine. Toss to thoroughly combine.

Turn into a 9-inch pie plate. Press onto bottom and up sides to form a firm, even crust. Bake in a 375° oven for 4 to 6 minutes. Cool thoroughly on wire rack.

1 **12-ounce can pear nectar**
1 **tablespoon cornstarch**
1 **teaspoon vanilla**

● Meanwhile, for glaze, in a saucepan combine pear nectar and cornstarch. Cook and stir over medium heat till thickened and bubbly. Cook and stir 2 minutes longer. Stir in vanilla. Set aside.

2 **tablespoons lemon juice**
1 **tablespoon water**
2 **small bananas, sliced**
2 **cups sliced fresh pears**
2 **cups fresh strawberries, sliced**
½ **of a small cantaloupe, seeded, sliced, and peeled**
**Whole strawberries (optional)**

● To assemble pie, in small bowl combine the lemon juice and the water. Dip the banana and pear slices in the lemon juice mixture, being careful not to mash the bananas.

Into prebaked crust, layer *¼ cup* of the glaze, the banana slices, another *¼ cup* of the glaze, the sliced strawberries, and another *¼ cup* of the glaze.

Arrange pear and cantaloupe slices atop glaze. Top with remaining glaze mixture. Chill 2 to 4 hours. Garnish with whole strawberries, if desired. Serves 8.

**For an easy piecrust, reach for the whole grain cereal box and a jar of toasted wheat germ. It's a twist on the familiar graham cracker crust. Fill it full of naturally sweet fresh fruit for a refreshing dessert. Or, substitute any of your favorite custard or ice cream fillings.**

# Barley Pudding

| 2 | slightly beaten egg yolks |
| 1¼ | cups cooked barley (see cooking directions, page 9) |
| ¾ | cup chopped mixed dried fruits |
| ½ | cup milk |
| 2 | tablespoons sugar |
| 2 | tablespoons butter *or* margarine, melted |
| ½ | teaspoon vanilla |

● In bowl stir together the beaten egg yolks, the cooked barley, the chopped mixed dried fruits, the milk, the sugar, the 2 tablespoons melted butter or margarine, and the vanilla. Set aside.

**Dress up barley for dessert in this baked custardlike pudding. The rolled oat topper adds a bit of crunch and extra sweetness.**

| 2 | egg whites |

● Beat egg whites to stiff peaks (tips stand straight). Fold egg whites into barley mixture. Turn mixture into six 6-ounce custard cups.

| ¼ | cup rolled oats |
| 2 | tablespoons finely chopped pecans |
| 1 | tablespoon brown sugar |
| 1 | tablespoon butter *or* margarine, melted |
| ⅛ | teaspoon ground cloves |

● In small bowl combine rolled oats, chopped pecans, brown sugar, the 1 tablespoon melted butter or margarine, and the ground cloves. Sprinkle evenly atop barley mixture in cups.

● Place custard cups in a 13x9x2-inch baking pan. Pour boiling water into pan around cups to a depth of 1 inch. Bake in a 325° oven for 20 to 25 minutes. Cool pudding in custard cups on wire rack. Serve pudding warm or chilled. Makes 6 servings.

# Grain-Fruit Pudding

1½ **cups milk**
½ **cup quick-cooking barley**
   ***or*** ⅓ **cup millet**

● In a heavy saucepan combine milk and barley or millet. Cook, covered, over low heat for 30 to 40 minutes till barley is tender and milk is absorbed; stir often (add more milk if necessary; mixture should be very thick).

2 **tablespoons honey**
½ **teaspoon vanilla**
¼ **cup coarsely chopped pecans**
¼ **cup mixed dried fruits, finely chopped**
¼ **cup shredded coconut**

● Stir in the honey and the vanilla. Add the coarsely chopped pecans, the chopped mixed dried fruits, and the shredded coconut. Cover and chill.

½ **cup whipping cream**
**Raspberry Sauce (see recipe, right)**

● Before serving, whip cream to soft peaks; fold into barley mixture. Spoon into sherbet dishes or wineglasses. Drizzle each serving with Raspberry Sauce. Makes 6 to 8 servings.

**Raspberry Sauce:** Reserve for garnish a few raspberries from one 10-ounce package thawed *frozen sweetened raspberries*. In saucepan crush remaining berries. Stir in 2 teaspoons *cornstarch*. Cook and stir till thick and bubbly. Cook and stir 2 minutes more. Sieve sauce; discard seeds. Cover sauce; cool to room temperature. Drizzle over pudding. Top with reserved berries. Makes about ⅔ cup.

# Index